Praise for *Civilizing the State*

John Restakis confronts one of the most important and neglected issues of our time. The nation state as we know it is an obsolete institution. With compelling and authoritative examples *Civilizing the State* lays out the problem and tests the solutions. An essential read for everyone concerned about the human future.

— David Korten, author, *When Corporations Rule the World* and *The Great Turning: From Empire to Earth Community*

As reactionary forces surge to the fore, John Restakis offers a bold vision for reinventing the state as a partner of the social economy, commons, and grassroots democracy. Thoughtful, provocative, and hopeful.

— David Bollier, commons activist and scholar, co-author, *Free, Fair, and Alive*

Could a better society be taking shape amidst the shards of our currently suicidal civilization? John Restakis makes a persuasive case that it is. He takes readers back to antiquity and up through intriguing experiments in our own time to explain that to solve the global crisis of the liberal state we must broaden, deepen, and enrich self-government. In *Civilizing the State*, readers will find both illumination and hope.

— Nancy MacLean, William H. Chafe Distinguished Professor of History and Public Policy, Duke University, author, *Democracy in Chains: The Deep History of the Radical Right's Stealth Plan for America*

These are times of fragmentation and despair, where we sorely need concrete utopias that can inspire us to construct the successor civilization. This record of our times provides grounds for optimism as we navigate the meta-crisis of civilization by linking grounded dreams to practical action. From the radical municipalism of Barcelona to the stateless democracy of Rojava, John Restakis gives us a portrait of partner state solutions that make possible the individual and social autonomy that we need in these critical times.

— Michel Bauwens, director and founder, P2P Foundation, co-author, *Peer to Peer: The Commons Manifesto*

John Restakis' *Civilizing the State* is a timely and necessary book in these times of corporate hijack of the state through neoliberal globalization. Three decades of deregulation have transformed welfare states "for the people, of the people, by the people" into corporate states "for the corporations, of the corporations, by the corporations." Nation states run by corporations for privatization of the commons and public goods are now mutating into corporate, surveillance states. Through examples of practice of direct democracy and political philosophies of civic participation, Restakis shows how we can reclaim democracy and the commons and shape a future for the common good.

— Vandana Shiva, ecological scientist, activist, founder, Research Foundation for
Science Technology and Ecology and Navdanya, founding board member,
International Forum on Globalisation, author, *Earth Democracy* and *Oneness Vs. the 1%*

This book will transform how you think about politics and power. The "partner state" breaks through the tiring squabbles about less or more government—instead, the question becomes how government can enable thicker, richer democracy in everyday life. Through stories that are both practical and radical, John Restakis introduces us to the politics we need for the 21st century.

— Nathan Schneider, professor and journalist, author, *Everything for Everyone:
The Radical Tradition that Is Shaping the Next Economy*
and *Thank You, Anarchy: Notes from the Occupy Apocalypse*

John Restakis' *Civilizing the State* deserves careful consideration. It is informative, perceptive, and persuasive. The book explores the notion of the common good and critically examines the role of democratic politics in enhancing cooperative behavior. A thorough expert in cooperative economics, Restakis gives the reasons why we need to civilize the state if we want to avert the risks of authoritarian governments, crony capitalism, and populisms of various sorts that threaten democracy. The type of politics which this book proposes is founded on the refusal of singularism and on the affirmation that rights cannot be separated from duties. This book is a must read for anyone who desires to think seriously about the future of our societies, freeing ourselves from some of our principal contemporary illusions.

— Stefano Zamagni, economics professor, University of Bologna,
author, *History of Economic Thought* and *Civil Economy*

CIVILIZING THE STATE

CIVILIZING THE STATE

RECLAIMING POLITICS FOR THE COMMON GOOD

JOHN RESTAKIS

new society
PUBLISHERS

Cover design by Diane McIntosh.
Cover image ©iStock

Printed in Canada. First printing November, 2021.

Inquiries regarding requests to reprint all or part of *Civilizing the State* should be addressed
to New Society Publishers at the address below. To order directly from the publishers,
please call toll-free (North America) 1-800-567-6772, or order online at www.newsociety.com

Any other inquiries can be directed by mail to:

New Society Publishers
P.O. Box 189, Gabriola Island, BC V0R 1X0, Canada
(250) 247-9737

Library and Archives Canada Cataloguing in Publication

Title: Civilizing the state : reclaiming politics for the common good / John Restakis.

Names: Restakis, John, author.

Description: Includes bibliographical references and index.

Identifiers: Canadiana (print) 20210270136 | Canadiana (ebook) 20210270209 |
ISBN 9780865719439 (softcover) | ISBN 9781550927368 (PDF) | ISBN 9781771423328 (EPUB)

Subjects: LCSH: Cooperation. | LCSH: Democracy. | LCSH: Common good. |
LCSH: State, The. | LCSH: Civil society.

Classification: LCC HD2963 .R45 2021 | DDC 334—dc23

New Society Publishers' mission is to publish books that contribute in fundamental ways
to building an ecologically sustainable and just society, and to do so with the least possible
impact on the environment, in a manner that models this vision.

Contents

Acknowledgments

Over the course of writing this book, I have been assisted by friends and colleagues whose reading and critical feedback of the early drafts have helped immeasurably in improving the text. Special thanks are due to Stefano Zamagni, Trebor Scholz, Vasilis Kostakis, David Korten, Nathan Schneider, Michel Bauwens, Ana Maria Peredo, Guy Dauncey, Kevin Flanagan, Leman Heseno, Ed Mayo, and Henry Tam. I am also deeply indebted to my colleagues and co-conspirators, Mike Lewis, Mike Gismondi, and Pat Conaty at Synergia Institute whose friendship and collaboration have so enriched my own analysis and understanding of the patterns that underlie the converging crises with which human society is confronted. It is a reminder that the solidarity and friendship of fellow travelers is as crucial to remaking the world as the values which drive us to the effort.

INTRODUCTION

T HERE ARE MOMENTS that define an epoch. Such a moment came on January 6, 2021, when white supremacists, incited by Donald Trump, broke through police barriers and stormed the U.S. Capitol. The world watched in disbelief as the doors to the House chamber were barricaded and members of Congress fled for safety while Trump supporters, sporting confederate flags and fascist insignia, roamed the halls looking for legislators they had branded as "traitors." Some had come with zip-tie cuffs to take hostages and hang those who had opposed Trump's efforts to overturn the presidential election. Outside the Capitol, a gallows had been built, complete with noose. Vice President Mike Pence and House Speaker Nancy Pelosi were high on their hit list.

Stunning images have emerged from that harrowing day. Some show the assembled mass thronging the steps and plaza of the Capitol building. Others show men in tactical gear scaling the perimeter walls. The image that best captures the *esprit* of the moment is that of 60-year-old Richard Barnett, a gun rights advocate from Arizona, lounging in the chair of the House Speaker, one boot propped on her desk, his grizzled face smiling in satisfaction. Before leaving, he scrawled a warning: "We will not back down." The insurgents rampaged through the Capitol for three hours, rifling through offices and defecating on the floors before walking out calmly, snapping selfies as police ushered them out like it was closing time at the Louvre. It was lost on no one that had this been a crowd of black

1

or brown people, the Capitol would have been turned into a killing field. By the end of the day, five people lost their lives and a nation no longer recognized itself.

To most, the insolence and the violence were appalling. However, Barnett and millions of others like him see themselves as patriots. The insurrection of January 6 was the bursting of an abscess that has been growing in the U.S. for years. Trump merely brought it to a head. The taking of the Capitol by fascists tore asunder the national myth of America. It traumatized a nation. But the U.S. was only the most recent country to be shaken by the rage of its citizens and the cynicism of its leaders.

On the morning following the 2019 EU elections, the French populace also awoke to a radically altered political reality. In a country that had come to symbolize the ideals of liberal democracy, Marine Le Pen's far-right National Rally Party had won the European elections, eclipsing the centrist party of French President Emmanuel Macron. Fuelled by a campaign of anti-immigrant rhetoric and the promise of jobs and "France for the French," the appeal of Le Pen's neo-fascist message had been gaining ground steadily among the country's bitter and growing underclass. As one supporter put it, "the veiled ones receive everything, and the French have nothing. It's not normal. Before, there was the rich, the middle class, and the poor. Now you have the rich and the poor. There is no longer any middle."[1]

Le Pen is not alone. As in France, the disappearing middle class in other European countries, not to mention the U.S., has resulted in the collapse of middle-of-the-road politics in Italy, Greece, Germany, Austria, the U.K., Sweden, The Netherlands, and Hungary. People are no longer content with the traditional safe solutions that reflect the status quo. Far-right figures are emerging victorious from Britain to Brazil. In India, Narendra Modi has marshalled a brand of Hindu fascism to wreak havoc in the world's largest democracy. In the U.S., far from rejecting the rising tide of fascism, the 2020 elections revealed a divided nation in which Donald Trump exerts a satanic spell on half the voting population.

But the political picture that is emerging from these events is not so clear-cut. The unprecedented electoral success of the Greens in these same European countries is evidence of a polarizing trend that has been growing for a decade. The mood is angry, volatile, insurrectionary. Political parties and the institution of government itself are deeply suspect. People are voting for change; for a shakeup of the old order. The more radical the political rhetoric, the more in keeping it is with the temper of the times. And in countries such as Portugal, Spain, Finland, Mexico, Bolivia, and New Zealand, political programs that are bold and unapologetic about challenging the status quo from a progressive perspective are also finding a ready audience. In his first address to Congress, Joe Biden explicitly rejected neoliberalism, asserted the centrality of government to the public welfare and announced the most ambitious program of social and economic reforms since the New Deal. His proposals for free college, a universal preschool program, an elder-care program, support for unions, and massive investment in public infrastructure found favour with 80 percent of viewers. Even 40 percent of *Republicans* supported his plan.[2] This signals a momentous ideological shift for America.

Central to these successes is a vision of government and the state that is in direct opposition to the neutered and passive role that has come to define the state over the last forty years. Moreover, the thirst for change has triggered a global groundswell of protest that is being felt from Asia to South America. As I write these lines, demands for radical system change are shaking governments in France, Hong Kong, Thailand, Lebanon, Iran, Iraq, Ecuador, Chile, Honduras, Haiti, Colombia, Peru, Bolivia, and the list is growing. In Chile, where neoliberalism first took shape under the dictatorship of Augusto Pinochet in the 1970s, the government came under siege to dismantle the capital-friendly policies that have since been replicated in every corner of the globe. The U.S., coming late to the party, finally exploded in a wave of protests not seen since the days of the civil rights movement. Against the backdrop of a pandemic that was out of control, the police killing of George Floyd marked a flashpoint in which widespread disgust over racism was soon transfigured into protest over the system and the status quo that perpetuates it.

In the current maelstrom of political upheaval, the ships of state that have offered direction and refuge in times of crisis are themselves in turmoil, rudderless, seemingly helpless to address the deep-seated fears that are radicalizing populations across the globe. From the destruction of social safety nets, to rising levels of debt and declining living standards, to the catastrophic effects of global warming, governments have been abdicating any meaningful role in providing the kind of determined leadership or direction that could conceivably meet such global threats head-on. Disillusion with the state as the steward of public welfare is deepening—and with good reason. From this vacuum of state leadership, there has arisen a resurgence of the right *and* demands for radical reform on the left. These are the twin forces unleashed by a global capitalist imperium that has set the world on a suicide course to extinction.

These deep systemic issues of collective life and the role of the state have now taken center stage as the world grapples with a pandemic. When I began writing this book in the fall of 2019, the issues described above were reaching a trigger point. But the coronavirus contagion and the skyrocketing fatalities have further exposed the dysfunction of our political economy. By the time this book comes out, the virus in the U.S. will have claimed 600,000 souls. The failures of the capitalist state are evident in the stark differences between those countries where the common welfare is still a principle of government and those in which the rule of markets reigns supreme. Measures that were unthinkable and would have been dismissed as radical and socialist before the contagion are now being deployed by governments to keep economies from tanking and to reassure a fearful and precarious citizenry. Discussions of a universal basic income (UBI) have now gone mainstream.

Everyone is confronting what it means when a state doesn't have a functioning public health system, when food and essential supplies are imported from half a world away, and when the economy is managed by a billionaire class that feeds off a vast and growing precariat. The failures of a broken system have come into full view, and the sense that something fundamental has to change is pervasive. What has also come into public consciousness, felt now as never before, is the interconnectivity of the world. Every individual on the planet is susceptible to what the pandemic is doing and feels the consequences of the choices made—or not made—as much by their government as by their next-door neighbour. We are in this together, and the reality of this fact has shifted from abstraction to lived personal experience.

What does this mean for the path ahead?

The empire of capital has split the world into two great and opposing forces: the upperworld of wealth and global civil society. But the seismic struggle for change extends far beyond politics and economics. The turmoil that is playing out in the world is as much a crisis of the spirit as it is of failed systems. The anguished calls for reform are not merely for changes of policy or political direction. They are the birth spasms of a new system of values and a vision of human community that are struggling to be born. The globalization of capitalism has not only engendered the injustices that are mobilizing populations to resistance. The projection of human power and greed on a global scale has ruptured the balance between humanity and the world's life systems. Ecosystem collapse is demanding a level of global response that is unprecedented. Change in our time means *transformation*. And while right wing populism appeals to the authoritarian tropes of the past, the struggle to fashion a real alternative to the status quo entails an altogether different, and more challenging, path forward. A fully sovereign and transfigured civil society—from local neighborhood to global stage—is at the heart of this vision.

It is an act of radical hope to strive for change in our times, and it is born of radical necessity. We are living through a crucible moment. What is done or left undone today will mark the future in indelible ways. And if we remain passive, if we are immobilized by cynicism, it is a future whose contours are already legible for those who care to read it.

For very many of us, the worry and unease we feel are reinforced daily by the echo chambers we inhabit online and from whence we receive our increasingly controlled sense of the world around us. We can feel the anxiety building on the streets of the world, on the lighted screens of our laptops, and in our bones. But what we are exposed to is a distorted and truncated view of things. Too often, we are left in the dark about those stories that reflect an altogether different picture of the world and of the people who are forging pathways for change that are both hopeful and indispensable if we are to navigate the uncertain terrain ahead. For this journey, we need an entirely different vision of what the future may hold and the pathways that may lead us there.

The threats posed by the politics of the status quo and its defenders are now not merely a question of political ideology or even of class. They have morphed into an existential threat to the survival of any form of humane civilization at all. The appearance of the coronavirus is like a call for an awakening.

I believe that the scope of the change that is needed is profound. A transformative vision that is equal to the challenges we now face as a species is not merely an accumulation of incremental steps within the current setup. It is to understand and relate to the world in an entirely different way and to fashion a political order that reclaims and elevates those attributes in us that have always been the foundation of humane societies. Co-operation and the instinctive bonds that unite us with each other and with the natural world are central to this vision. The task of politics now is to make such a vision manifest.

My aim in this book is to expand on some key themes I introduced in *Humanizing the Economy: Co-operatives in the Age of Capital*. In that work, I attempted to show how a set of values based on democracy, co-operation, social justice, and the pursuit of the common good could, *and are*, being realized daily in the practice of co-operative economics the world over. In the work that follows, my aim is to show the implications of these values for the broader questions of political economy that are essential if we wish to alter the suicide course we are on.

My underlying hypothesis is that a deepening of democracy and co-operation for the common good are the only means by which the changes we seek might be realized. Contrary to the individualism and self-interest that sustain the capitalist worldview, the common good proposes an alternative framework for our political aims and a pathway through the crisis of legitimacy that imperils democracy itself. Both these tendencies—co-operation for common benefit and competition for self-interest—are embedded in every human society. How the human species handles these contending forces will determine the future that lies in store—for people and planet alike. But the values I treat here also deal with issues of spiritual renewal. I hope to show that co-operation and the common good are both the manifestation *and the means* by which a transformative vision of human community—and human consciousness—is made real.

The civilizing values that are the foundation of humane societies are present in every community. They have been with us always. The forms they take are prismatic. Like a light source refracted through the prism of time and place and culture, their manifestations in the world of politics are as various as the circumstances in which they are applied. Their realization is a continuous—and collective—labor of social and spiritual evolution.

The roles of the state and of civil society are at the center of this story. If the state has abandoned its duty as steward of the common welfare, if it has betrayed the only purpose that gives it legitimacy, it has not done so accidentally. And if the average citizen is left confused and uncertain of his or her place in the larger scheme of their community or country, it is the price we pay for the catastrophic erosion of the social values and basic trust that binds communities together. This, too, is a vacuum that is exploited by the demagogues of nationalism, of ethnicity and tribal identity whose politics serve not to heal and unite, but to sow hatred and division.

We seek something better. And, contrary to the fatalist's view that there is nothing to be done, that all politics is the same, that one government is as bad as the next, we will point to those examples that show how a different kind of politics and a different view of the future is possible. It is a hope that burns in the breasts of the millions that have been marching for change the world over. And, as the world confronts the consequences of a deadly pandemic, the deep reservoir of co-operation and concern for the common welfare that sustains all societies will be the key to weathering this crisis, as with every previous crisis.

Ultimately, this book is a work of hope and perhaps a torch in darkening times. I do not hide my sense that what I share here is also a work of experimentation—an extended reflection on what a very particular set of beliefs and values discloses when we begin to take them seriously as a foundation for a new political order. Nor do I hide my own ambivalence about whether such a vision as I present here is at all likely to be realized in the near future, or at all. But that isn't the point.

Those who dreamt and fought for the ideals of democracy, lib-. erty, and equality in the time of monarchs were indispensable precisely *because* their hopes seemed so distant to the times. They were torchbearers. They called upon values in the human condition that are innate in all people and all societies. These same values are vibrant and alive today, and it is precisely their violation that I believe is fuelling much of the rage and resentment we now witness. The task before us is to take up these same values and to invest them with the power and the means to remake the world in their image. What is this image?

That is the purpose of this book.

I have structured the narrative in three sections. The first three chapters set out the nature of the task before us. They include the historical and political antecedents to the present moment, to the formation of the political and economic powers that govern our present condition, to the systemic plunder of the planet's commons, and to the deepening crisis of legitimacy that has sparked resistance and reaction the world over.

The middle section delves into the ways in which widely divergent communities are remaking their politics and economics to reflect their vision of democratic governance and the pursuit of the common good. From the mass uprisings of the *Indignados* movement in Spain to the Kurd's battle for survival in the bedlam of Syria, these are also stories of bitter struggle in the face of seemingly impossible odds. As far as possible, I try and situate these stories in their political and historical context and extrapolate general principles from the particulars of the case. The examples here establish a bridge to the final section of the book.

The closing section attempts a synthesis of the ideas, values, models, and practices that together frame a vision of political economy and the relationship between citizenry and the state that offers a new narrative for the necessary work that lies ahead, and perhaps a compass to guide us toward the foundational aims we hold in common. A central theme in this section is an elaboration on the idea of the Partner State, which frames a new understanding of the state from the perspective of a sovereign society and the precepts of civil economy.

We are not alone in this work. People the world over are striving to realize a set of values that have always been at the foundation of humane communities and the source of sustenance and well-being for people in every age and every place. The recovery and reinterpretation of these values today is a matter of personal happiness, of human welfare, of reframing social purpose to preserve what is best in us and to treasure and protect the abounding beauty of the world around us.

I read once that what humankind dreams it is compelled to realize in real life.[3] We are called upon to dream well. Now, it is a matter of survival.

TREASON OF THE STATE[1]

O N THE SWELTERING SUMMER day of August 22, 1996, Bill Clinton signed into law the most momentous change to U.S. social policy since the passage of FDR's Social Security Act in 1935. The Personal Responsibility and Work Opportunity and Reconciliation Act promised to "end welfare as we know it." Indeed, it did. Surrounded by cabinet members and American flags on the sunlit lawn of the White House, Clinton abolished the Aid to Families with Dependent Children program (AFDC)—the primary safety net protecting poverty-stricken mothers and children—and replaced it with the Temporary Aid to Needy Families program (TANF). The sign in front of him bore the slogan A New Beginning—Welfare to Work. It was a fitting sentiment to characterize this monumental shift in social policy.

Among the group standing next to him on that day was Lillie Harden, a 42-year-old black woman from Little Rock, Arkansas. Clinton had met Harden on a panel ten years earlier. Impressed by her story, Clinton invited her to tell how her own escape from welfare was due to the welfare-to-work policies that he had implemented in Arkansas while he was governor. In her speech, Harding recounted how she had used AFDC while unemployed for two years, until enrolling in one of Clinton's workfare programs and landing a minimum-wage job as a kitchen helper. She remarked how important this was to her as a badge of success and the recovery of her self-esteem: "When I got my job, my son was so proud of me, but I made a deal with him, I told him, I'm going to work every day and take my work seriously."

Harden, and her carefully crafted image as a reformed "welfare queen," was central to Clinton's success that day. Her presence bolstered Clinton's credentials as a compassionate reformer. It also gave credence to the image of the "welfare queen" peddled by Republicans. From the time Ronald Reagan used "welfare queens" to portray the poor as living off other people's money, Republicans have attacked welfare as an entitlement program that rewarded the lazy and the irresponsible. The image of the unwed black mother breeding children and sponging off welfare—an archetype of the undeserving poor—was embedded in the American imagination.

The passage of TANF in the U.S. was to inaugurate a new era of personal responsibility and hard work as the answer to systemic poverty. With the steep reduction in federal funding that followed, and the shifting of responsibility for the new program to the states, the federal government's role for the welfare of its citizens was not so much a new beginning as a return to a dismal past where the poor were blamed for their poverty.

This focus on personal responsibility (or lack thereof) as the root cause of poverty had been a principle of faith for Republicans and the right since the earliest days of the republic. It was balanced in their minds by the myth of personal merit as the root cause of wealth. Cynically believing that it would win him votes and neutralize Republicans in the coming elections, Clinton embraced it for the Democrats as well. It was a turning point for the Democratic Party and for the country.

Following her brief speech at the signing ceremony, Lillie Harden was forgotten, and she melted back into the obscurity from which she had emerged momentarily on that hot August day. But her story continued, invisible, unremarked, and ultimately ending as a tragic commentary on the policies she had praised and to which she would eventually fall victim. After suffering a stroke in 2002, Harden was no longer able to qualify for Medicaid as she had under AFDC, or to afford her monthly prescriptions. In the end, like millions of other poor black women, Lillie lost the frail protection of the old welfare program in return for the promised benefits a job would bring to her and her family. Leaving behind three children, she died in poverty an agonizing twelve years later at the age of 59.[2]

Lillie Harden's story, and the circumstances of her brief appearance in the public eye, embody all that is irremediably wrong with the state of politics and public life today, not only in the U.S., but across a wide swathe of the capitalist world. It is not merely that the brief progress of social welfare in the postwar era had come to an ignoble end. There has always been opposition to the notion that the state has any responsibility in providing for the poor or indeed for the public welfare. It is the basis of the neoliberal ideas that now dominate public policy the world over.

But the rolling back of public programs, whether for the protection of the poor or for investment in education or health care, would not have been possible without the collusion of political parties that sold out the very people they claimed to represent. It was a betrayal born of cynicism, of political calculation, of the abandonment of principle, and, ultimately, of the absence of any progressive vision with which to oppose the disastrous free market ideology that was the driving force of a resurgent right.

◆ ◆ ◆

The start of America's reluctant experimentation with welfare came at the height of the Great Depression when Franklin D. Roosevelt signed the Social Security Act as part of his New Deal program. When the Great Depression began, about 18 million of the elderly, the disabled, and single mothers with children already lived at a bare subsistence level in the United States. By 1933, more than 50 percent of the elderly were living in poverty,[3] and another 13 million Americans had been thrown out of work.[4]

The Social Security Act established a national welfare system aimed at poor children and other dependent persons, and from the very beginning, Republicans, as well as conservative Democrats, opposed it. Echoing the arguments used by corporations, opponents charged that the program was a "creeping socialism" that would destroy freedom, unfairly tax employers, and harm the economy. They were the same arguments that would later be used to attack the introduction of Medicare and Medicaid in 1965/66 and the Affordable Care Act in 2010. They are being used today to oppose the expansion of Medicare to universal coverage.

The charge of socialism was meant as a scare tactic, to be sure. But it pointed to a deeper conflict concerning the nature of government, its role as steward of the public welfare, and whether or not the state has any role to play in service to a common good. The issues raised in 1935 were hardly new. They go to the root of the relationship between state and society, and they are as pertinent today as they were then.

The origin of the modern welfare state dates to the improbable introduction of a national health insurance program in Germany by Otto von Bismarck, in 1883. With his walrus moustache and spiked helmet clapped to his bulldog head, Bismarck was not known for his democratic sensibilities or his social empathy. But this dour Prussian autocrat had a socialist problem. Revolutionary fervour had been sweeping the continent, culminating in the 1848 revolutions that affected 50 countries. It was a purely political calculation that led Bismarck to initiate a national health service to beat the socialists at their own game and to win popular support for the newly unified German state.[5]

Of Bismarck's intentions, historian Jonathan Steinberg noted, "It had nothing to do with social welfare. He just wanted some kind of bribery to get social democratic voters to abandon their party."[6] "Call it socialism or whatever you like," Bismarck said during the 1881 Reichstag debates. "It is the same to me."[7]

The German system provided retirement benefits as well as disability benefits. Participation was mandatory, and contributions were taken from the employee, the employer, and the government. Coupled with the workers' compensation program established in 1884 and the "sickness" insurance enacted the year before, the program provided a comprehensive system of income security based on social insurance principles.

The revolutions that had shaken Europe in 1848 haunted and terrified ruling elites. But Bismarck's social welfare strategy did not succeed in derailing the socialist threat. Socialist ideas continued to radicalize and mobilize large sections of the populace not only in Germany after 1883 but across the continent. The issue of class, of the misery of working life, of constant precariousness, and of the duty of the state to protect and provide for its citizens remained at the forefront of political struggle across the continent.

With the arrival of the Industrial Revolution and the rise of an urban working class came the struggle for trade unions and worker protections, the fight for universal suffrage, and the push for an interventionist state. These became essential components of the socialist project in Europe and beyond. The co-operative societies of the early industrial era were the seedbeds of socialism, trade unionism, women's rights, and the push for the radical economic and political reforms that defined the shape and direction of political struggle down to our own time. The primary battleground for this struggle was the state—its purpose, its organization, and its control.

When Lenin wrote *The State and Revolution* in the summer of 1917, he believed that Europe was on the brink of revolution and that the dawning of a new age was at hand. Having fled from Petrograd to Finland to escape arrest, Lenin authored the book as a treatise to guide socialists on how to bring about a new political and economic order. It was written large, taking in the whole sweep of his political vision, and fuelled by a mixture of certainty, arrogance, contempt for his opponents, and exulting in the violence and destruction that a workers' revolution would require. In it, he made control of the state the pivotal point around which the future of the socialist revolution would turn.

The capture of the state by the working class was the first step that would pave the way for a transition from capitalism to communism, with the state eventually withering away as communism eliminated the exploitation of one class by another. This followed from the Marxist principle that the state was a bourgeois creation, a product of capitalism, and operated essentially as a mechanism for the control and oppression of the working class by the owners of capital. The elimination of class would lead naturally to the demise of the state. It did not lead to democracy. It led to a stateless dictatorship of the proletariat and the liquidation of the bourgeoisie.

For Lenin, the withering away of the state required the erasure of any distinction between the state as a governing apparatus and the population as a whole. It was a view of a society in which every member is required to become part of a single productive system, a "huge single syndicate" as Lenin put it, controlled and administered by a revolutionary party. It was, in short, a totalitarian vision.[8]

Oceans of ink have been devoted to the dissection and interpretation of this theory. Its influence in shaping the course of socialism and the politics of revolution in the 20th century is unparalleled. So too, is the suffering inflicted by its deficiencies as a theory of change and its consequences when put into practice. The view of the state as a mere by-product of capitalist economic forces is also wrong, contradicted by the evidence of history, archaeology, and anthropology and questioned even within the Marxist tradition.

Lenin's conception was premised on the idea that economics drives social order and that the conflict between classes necessitates the imposition of a control apparatus by the ruling minority upon the majority. It was a vision that accepted violence and competition as the natural order of society and was, in effect, a reverse image of the social Darwinism embraced by capitalism to justify this very inequality. Both Marx and Engels were admirers of Darwin and attributed to him the discovery in the natural world of the materialism they espoused in the historical evolution of society.[9]

For anyone studying history, it is hard to deny the hard kernel of truth embedded in this vision. But unlike Marx's view, Darwin's theory is not teleological. Natural selection is a never-ending process with no ultimate end point. The Marxist conviction that the strife between classes will ultimately end with the collapse of capitalism and the triumph of a communist society is, in effect, the end of historical evolution.[10]

Darwin's theory of natural selection, and its immense relevance to political theory, was heavily influenced by the Victorian ethos and the competitive individualism that dominated the economic and political ideology of the time. This was, after all, the era that established laissez-faire capitalism as the template for human progress. Competition for survival was accepted as the driving force of evolution. But this view did not go unchallenged.

An opposing view of the natural world and the evolution of human society was proposed by Peter Kropotkin, a contemporary of Marx and one of the founding fathers of anarchism. For Kropotkin, co-operation and mutual aid were as much a part of the natural order as competition and the bloody violence of nature as described by Darwin. Kropotkin, a member of the Russian aristocracy and a hereditary prince, was an esteemed scientist whose work on the geology and geography of Siberia placed him in the front rank of the scientific community. But it was his research into the survival tactics of animal species and the publication of *Mutual Aid: A Factor of Evolution*, in 1902, that earned him his place as a leading figure in both the anarchist and co-operative traditions. His investigations into the prevalence of co-operation in animal species offered a compelling case against the competitive individualism that characterized the Darwinian worldview and the economic and political theories of both capitalism and socialism that were based on it.

Mutual Aid became a seminal work for a long line of research and theory on the evolution of natural systems and also of human societies, economic systems, and politics. This work, and the stream of co-operative thought that flowed from it, have lain buried and neglected to this day. It was only in 2009, when Elinor Ostrom won the Nobel Prize for her ground-breaking studies on the commons, that serious interest in co-operation was reignited and a window thrown open to this forgotten legacy. Her work on the commons upended two centuries of bias concerning collective governance and the co-operative use of resources. Its significance for understanding the organization of human societies and the implications of co-operative and commons theory for system change is impossible to overstate.

To advocates of co-operation, Ostrom's confirmation that human societies all over the world successfully manage resources held in common was old news. But in this present moment of global crisis and the competitive individualism that drives it, the work of Ostrom, Kropotkin, and other thinkers in the co-operative and commons tradition is a crucial resource for rethinking how human societies work, the values that shape them, and our understanding of what is possible for the future.

There is a certain folly in grafting evidence from the natural world onto the human experience and the conduct of human society. For nothing is more clear than that humankind is distinguished from the natural world precisely *because* of our capacity to act in ways that, if anything, contradict the natural behavior of other species to the point of undermining even our own prospects for survival. The human condition is not fixed. Our circumstances are as much a consequence of our actions as are the external pressures of place and environment. Global warming, the extermination of other animal species, the incessant wars, and the ecocide we are practicing are terrifying cases in point. What is also true is that the propensities for co-operation and competition are hardwired into our makeup, just as they are in the natural world.

Darwin and Kropotkin were both right. Co-operation and competitive individualism are not mutually exclusive. They are the twin poles of the natural order. Human society is evidence of that. But to a very large extent, how human societies evolve, how our political systems and power relations are constructed, and how we understand and interact with each other and our environment is a matter of choice. There are biological determinants, to be sure. But how we live them out in the context of human society is in our hands. The challenge before us is how to draw upon and strengthen those elements in our human makeup—both individually and socially—that conduce to the humanist values we espouse.

If we trace the evolution of human societies from the earliest evidence, it is astonishing how recent are the patterns of social life that we now take for granted. This is most evident in how we perceive our forms of governance. The organization of human societies into states appears only around 2,600 BCE with the city of Uruk, in ancient Mesopotamia. With a population of about 25,000, Uruk was the earliest example of what may be considered the basic matrix of the state: an agricultural economy based on grain and fixed field farming, social stratification and specialization, control over a specified territory, an armed force, taxation, and walls.

Slaves and the domination of a ruling elite were also characteristic of Uruk, and of early states from Mesopotamia to Southeast Asia and China.[11] The later city-states of classical Greece, which we take as models of democracy, were slave states where the rights of citizenship excluded women and, obviously, slaves.[12] Indeed, as James C. Scott has suggested, the process of domestication that was the foundation of the hierarchical state was not restricted to plants and animals. It extended equally to humans.[13] Human domestication and the natural impulse to resistance represent the antipodes of a perennial struggle between domination and freedom.

The state became, and remains, the basic framework within which human societies play out the dynamics of group conflict on the one hand and collective needs on the other. However, all nation-states are also a form of deception. Like the individual ego, the state is an abstraction constructed through the simplification and idealization of a set of attributes selectively chosen by those powers that are able to impose them. These attributes may be linguistic, cultural, historical, religious, racial, political, or any combination of these and others. The nation-state exists via a simultaneous act of inclusion and exclusion, of belonging and alienation, of acceptance and rejection. Like all identities, nation-states are defined equally by what they embrace as by what they reject as "other." The exclusion or repression of difference is in their makeup. But above all, the state as we know it is validated by its monopoly on power and the submission to this power by its subjects.

It was not until the 18th century that democracy was seriously advanced by the Enlightenment philosophers as a mortal challenge to the hierarchical systems of church and monarchy that defined the nation-states in Europe and the colonial territories they controlled. Democracy, as we have come to understand it, is a very late arrival on the historical stage. And, as events unfolding around us testify, it is an open question what role it will ultimately play or for how long. Historically, democracy appears as an exotic plant amidst a forest of authoritarian political forms, ranging from local dynasties, to regional theocracies, to monarchic empires. Today, despite its promising expansion in the late 20th century, its existence remains fragile, under threat, with its institutions in retreat globally.[14]

However constructed, the form of politics that a society creates is ultimately a function of how power is accumulated, deployed, and, above all, in whose benefit. The perpetual interplay of social versus personal interest is central to this process. This is as true of human societies as it is of the natural world. These observations may strike one as banal, but the interplay of the social versus the individual, of co-operation versus competition, and the manner in which a political system manages this fundamental dualism is the basis of all political economy and a key to understanding the vast ebb and flow of political systems. Moreover, it is not a case of assigning a superior moral value to one element over the other—social and individual identities are essential components in the human makeup.

What concerns us is how political systems mitigate, or magnify, the damage done by those human impulses that, left unchecked, destroy the quality of life—the prospects for happiness—both for individuals and societies. Chief among these is the lust for power, *titonolatry*, and the greed and selfishness that it fosters. Power in this sense is an instrument of predation. Those who pursue it are those least to be trusted with it. The pursuit of power for its own sake is a social pathology that manifests at the level both of the individual and class. The case I want to make is that democracy is essentially a system to mitigate this damage through the broadest possible diffusion of political power. It is a process of political dilution. Whether operating at the level of consensual decision-making at the scale of the tribe in times past or acting as a check on the power of elites at national or even global levels today, democracy is society's way of protecting itself against the abuses of its most predatory members.

Marxism addressed this by identifying capitalist owners of property as a predatory class feeding off an exploited working class. This is not far wrong. But it overlooked the fact that any group or class that exercises undisputed political power inevitably becomes an exploiting and predatory power. Contrary to Marxism's hopes, there is nothing inherently virtuous about the working class that would inoculate it against the abuse of power, should it ever attain it. Moreover, it does not suffice to speak of class interests when, in practice, it is always individuals that exercise power (ostensibly) on behalf of those interests. In worst-case scenarios, the monstrous appetites and disorders of the dictatorial personality supersede even class interests. Cases in point: Mao Zedong, Donald Trump.

This brings us to a second point concerning the actual operations of power in a supposedly egalitarian state. Engels himself recognized that the withering away of the state required the habituation of a population to live without the violence and subordination instilled by class oppression. But it is not solely class oppression that inspires in people the will to violence, to domination, or to subjection. In even the most egalitarian grouping of classless hunter-gatherers, we would not be surprised to find petty despots, bullies, or just your standard universal asshole. (As a human trait, assholery, we may safely assume, is classless, ubiquitous, and perpetual.)

Engels was certainly speaking of something more substantial in society, something *systemic* and *cultural* that required fixing, not isolated individual behaviors. It is true that the creation of a more just and egalitarian society requires a commensurate set of attitudes and behaviors on the part of its members. The essential question is, how does this come about? Changing political systems is difficult enough. Changing social attitudes is infinitely more so.

The standard account of social and political evolution is that humankind is engaged in an epic journey of progress, evolving from more barbarous to more civilized forms of social organization. This story—the myth of human progress—was a product of the revolutionary forces that were unleashed with the dawning of the Enlightenment, the age of reason. These were both intellectual and material.

The unhindered application of reason in philosophy and the scientific discoveries that made possible the material advancements of the Industrial Revolution combined to provide a compelling tale of progress in which reason guided the moral and material improvement of humankind. In politics, its crowning achievement was the triumph of liberal democracy, a natural consequence of this conviction. For if humanity's destiny lay in the cultivation of reason, and if everyone was endowed with it, the source of political legitimacy lay not with the divine right of kings or the inherited privileges of nobility but in the rational acts and free choices of the individual. It was a revolutionary myth, a storming of the gates of both religious and secular authority, and its effects were as evident in the collectivist salvation mythology of Marxism as they were in the individualist free market credo of capitalism. The idea of the state, its role and ultimate purpose, was molded by these mythologies.

But no myth is without its basis in human experience. And the historical experience of humankind with respect to politics, with the perpetual strife and suffering of domination and exploitation, may be read as a story of the survival and self-defence of societies against predatory minorities. Karl Polanyi formulated this process as a Double Movement, in which societies defend themselves against the violation of social norms and values by the unchecked operations of capital. It is a never-ending dance of power where an advance by one side prompts a counter response by the other. For the most part, Polanyi developed his metaphor to describe the dynamics of a market economy, or to be more accurate, a market *society*, in which social values are subordinated to those of the market. But this insight concerning the perpetual interplay between the interests of capital and those of society, different from the Marxist formulation of class struggle, may be expanded to account for a far wider conflict that is entailed in the notion of *social predation*.

From the vantage point of collective well-being, progress in politics ultimately entails the creation of mechanisms for the advancement of the common good, a conception that goes all the way back to Aristotle.[15] For humanists, who believe that happiness and well-being should not be the preserve of a privileged minority, government and the state must ultimately be judged against this criterion. This was the aim of the democratic revolutions that shook Europe throughout the 17th and 18th centuries and whose ideals are being fought for still.

This reading of democracy as a form of social self-defence, however, is incomplete. The democratic idea, after all, concerns itself not only with the collective welfare but equally with the freedom and welfare of the individual as a political subject, as a free citizen of a political community. In this sense, democracy was the means by which the individual could realize his/her potential to the fullest and through this process of self-realization society as a whole was advanced. Liberal democracy was defined by this, as was the capitalist system that developed symbiotically alongside it. These principles were encoded, in one form or another, in virtually every constitution of the modern era, with eighty-seven countries now formally constituted as democracies.

That the state should be bound by these claims of democracy, that governments should be held accountable for the fulfilment of these ideals—both social and individual—is the basis of political legitimacy in the modern era. From the establishment of the first constitutional republic in the U.S. in 1776 to the pronouncements of virtually every despotic regime from China to Chechnya, this appeal to the preservation and welfare of a nation's populace, even when contradicted in practice, remains the foundation of political legitimacy in every corner of the globe. If this is true, a betrayal of this trust constitutes a form of treason by the state for no state is bound by any such allegiance to any other group. This unique allegiance and identity with a political community is a foundational principle of the nation-state.

What happens when this rather comforting ideal is exposed as a farce? When a state betrays the trust of its citizens? When, contrary to the expectation of progress, of individual freedom or social justice, the old forms of privilege and plunder re-emerge stronger and more arrogant than ever? We are finding out.

The betrayal of America's postwar social contract with which we started our account is but one instance of state treason that is reversing the political covenant of nations with their citizens the world over. A key symptom of this is the steeply rising rates of inequality in virtually every region of the world—particularly in the U.S.—and the precipitous decline in public wealth and state investment in social welfare, especially in areas like education, health, housing, and public infrastructure.[16]

The appearance of the welfare state coincides with the rise of the mass movements that shook Europe during the revolutionary upheavals of the 17th and 18th centuries. The transition to democracy and the triumph of capitalism that followed on the collapse of the old aristocratic regimes amounted to a mutation in the social order. Politics as a deliberative process that included the whole of a society had now become possible. It did not eradicate the power of elites. But it did change the dynamics of social power. Democracy transformed the state from being a mechanism of monopoly control to a political arena where power could be contested. The state became a formalized field of struggle in which the whole of society was to play a part. In the process, the art of politics became infinitely more complex, utilizing aspects of human mass psychology and social manipulation that were previously unknown—precisely because they had been unnecessary in authoritarian regimes where power is legitimized not through the winning of popular consent but through the exercise of brute force.

The electoral process meant that the collective interests of a population, however conceived, might be realized through politics. These interests were bound up with directing the behavior of governments toward ends that conduced to the welfare of society as a whole, not simply the interests of elites. Chief among these was protection against the damaging effects of the capitalist system. Over the course of 150 years, roughly from the late 1700s to the middle of the 1900s, democracy became the primary means by which the rule of elites could be held in check by a population. It was the formalized instrument of collective power.

The rise of democracy coincides with the gradual introduction of programs that reflected this concern with social equality and the provision for individual and collective welfare. Conversely, the decline of democracy we are witnessing today entails exactly the opposite—the destruction of social welfare and the reassertion of privilege and inequality. This, in turn, requires the crippling of the state in its role as protector of the common welfare.

The conflict between the rights of private property and the common welfare is the central contradiction of the capitalist state. The reversal of policies that pay for the promotion of the common welfare is the main weapon in an arsenal aimed at the permanent disablement of government as an instrument of public power. Beginning in the U.K. and the U.S. during the Thatcher/Regan era, the rise of neoliberal policies spearheaded by tax cuts, public sector privatization, and "welfare reform," have now become dogma-driving economic and public policy across the globe. The collapse of social welfare through the imposition of austerity policies in country after country is ultimately an assault on the legitimacy of government as the protector of the common welfare. The privatization of public wealth and the colonization of the public sector by capital is an essential part of this process. Another is the glorification of the individual and the demonization of the social.

Social Murder

In his classic work, *The Condition of the Working Class in England*,[17] Engels recounted the manner in which capitalist social relations in Victorian England produced conditions that killed and maimed working people. He cited "a pretty list of diseases engendered purely by the hateful money-greed of the manufacturers. Women made unfit for childbearing, children deformed, men enfeebled, limbs crushed, whole generations wrecked, afflicted by disease and infirmity, purely to fill the purses of the bourgeoisie." These conditions included poor diets, alcohol consumption, shoddy housing, fetid and unsanitary crowding, disease, violence, and the premature deaths of working people. As the effects of the actions of the bourgeoisie were both foreseeable and avoidable, Engels argued, they could be construed as social murder:

> When one individual inflicts bodily injury upon another such injury that death results, we call the deed manslaughter; when the assailant knew in advance that the injury would be fatal, we call his [sic] deed murder. But when society places hundreds of proletarians in such a position that they inevitably meet a too early and an unnatural death, one which is quite as much a death by violence as that by the sword or bullet; when it deprives thousands of the necessaries of life, places them under conditions in which they cannot live—forces them, through the strong arm of the law, to remain in such conditions until that death ensues which is the inevitable consequence—knows that these thousands of victims must perish, and yet permits these conditions to remain, its deed is murder just as surely as the deed of the single individual.[18]

Social murder applies equally to the destruction of lives brought on by the austerity policies implemented by governments of all stripes and aimed at the so-called excesses of the welfare state and the benefits enjoyed by the idle and underserving poor. In Engel's time, these were the consequences of an industrial system that was fed by an unending stream of precarious human labor—uprooted, underpaid, and ultimately disposable. The mass uprisings of the 17th and 18th centuries sought to address these very conditions—initially through the introduction of democracy and, later, via the social protections of the welfare state. Today, the reversal of those victories in the name of austerity hearkens not only to a feudal past but to an equally frightening future.

What, then, might we make of regimes, such as those of Trump in the U.S. or Bolsonaro in Brazil, where the foreseeable and preventable deaths of hundreds of thousands are brought about by the deliberate deception of a populace and the neglect of basic protections against a global pandemic? Social murder seems an apt term.

Welfare "reform" and the disablement of government is the raison d'être of austerity. Always, it is the vulnerable individual and the programs that serve the weakest members of society that are in austerity's crosshairs—never the excesses of the rich or the uncountable (and untaxed) wealth that has swollen the coffers of the one percent and the corporations they control. Meanwhile, the Lillie Hardens of the world are legion and growing.

In her remarkable work, *Democracy in Chains*, historian Nancy MacLean chronicles this process of democratic dismemberment in depressing detail.[19] Unsurprisingly, the recent origins of this process, at least in the U.S., are bound up in the inequalities of race and the efforts of government to impose restrictions on the powers of capital.

It is in this wider context that we must construe the notion of civilizing the state—as a process of democratic reclamation that restores the legitimacy of the state by conforming its operations to the material *and social* well-being of its citizens. This, in turn, is a continuation of that democratizing process that conceived of the state as an instrument of collective welfare. In our time, given the realignment of roles and powers that this will require, we can call this reimagined polity a Partner State. What this entails in practice we will examine in the examples that follow and in the concluding chapters of the book.

CIVIL POWER AND
THE NEW LEGITIMACY

W HEN ONE VISITS modern-day Athens, it is impossible to
shake the sense that one is moving in a land haunted, perhaps even taunted, by its ghosts—those departed gods whose spirits
linger still in the shadowed recesses of the sun-washed temples, in
the quiet of the cypress groves, and in the timeless presence of their
marbled images. Up on the Acropolis rock, in the tourist high tide
of summer, the crowds overflow and spill down the hillside to the
theatre of Herod Atticus, to the bars and boutiques of the Plaka,
and to the ancient agora where Socrates held court.

Six hundred meters across from the Acropolis rises the pine-clad
hill of Philopappou. After ascending the stone-set path leading up
from the agora, one arrives at the Pnyx, a semicircular plateau built
upon the flank of the hill and sustained by a cyclopean wall of hewed
stone. It is 110 meters across, inclining gently to a stepped terrace
carved from the living bedrock, and built to hold up to 8,000 people.
Beginning in the 6th century BC, this was the meeting place of the
Athenian democratic assembly, the place where democracy in the
West was invented and where today, aside from a few wandering
souls and the rasping of the occasional crow, nothing stirs and si-
lence reigns.

If one wishes to be dramatic about it, one could say—with only
slight exaggeration—that politics as we know it begins here, on this
grassy promontory. Collective forms of consensual decision-making

have been practiced in human societies from time immemorial. However, it was here that the formal idea of civil power took shape, and its practice, if not perfected, was attempted with a thoroughness that remains unrivalled. The rise of civil power, its progress and regress, is a marker of political evolution itself. For politics, if it is to be anything more than the self-interested gang wars of elites, entails an engagement, a movement involving the whole of a community. It presupposes the existence of a civil society. Civil power meant the organized expression of a citizenry, a community of people with claims to political rights. Given its centrality in the themes we are developing, we should take a few moments to consider the history and significance of this idea in relation to political economy, the common good, and the current frame of world events.

The subject of civil society has spawned a huge literature. But it was the mass mobilizations that brought down the Berlin Wall, the USSR, and the satellite regimes of Eastern Europe that placed civil society at the center stage of global politics. To this day, civil mobilization on a mass scale has continued unabated. From global resistance to the WTO trade deals and the unfettered power of corporations in the 90s, to the movement for democracy in Tiananmen Square, to the Arab Spring, to the Occupy movement, to the student marches against global warming and Black Lives Matter, the mobilization of civil power is a constant, if discontinuous, expression of popular discontent. And, most significantly, it is taking place outside of the established political parties, of both left *and* right. In a very real sense, politics, both globally and locally, is being determined by this rising tide of discontent and the mass mobilizations that give it voice.

The term *civil society* appears in one of the earliest treatises we have on political theory, the *Politics* of Aristotle. But the meaning of the term has evolved, reflecting the shifts in philosophic thought, in systems of economic organization, in the evolution of political institutions, and in the ways that human culture itself has changed, particularly as a result of technology and modes of communication.

For Aristotle, civil society was quite simply a political community (*koinonia politike*), a community (*koinonia*) of citizens associated with a particular *polis*, or a Greek city-state. In Aristotle's usage, the adjective *politike* signifies "the art of the common life of the polis and the betterment of that life." In the Latin translation, *politike* became *civilis*, an adjective pertaining to a member of a city, hence the word *citizen*. Aristotle's *koinonia politike* was translated by writers of Latin as *societas civilis*, civil society.

Aristotle famously declared that man is a social animal, a political animal.[1] He naturally seeks to associate with other men, and all associations were purposeful—they existed because their members had mutual needs and common aims. While acknowledging that many kinds of associations existed, Aristotle claimed that political association was the highest form of association, encompassing all others, because political ends were the highest ends of man. As he says in *The Nicomachean Ethics*:

> All forms of community are like parts of the political community; for men journey together with a view to some particular advantage, and to provide something that they need for the purposes of life; and it is for the sake of advantage that the political community too seems both to have come together originally and to endure, for this is what legislators aim at, and they call just that which is to the common advantage. Now the other communities aim at advantage bit by bit, e.g., sailors at what is advantageous on a voyage with a view to making money or something of the kind or fellow soldiers at what is advantageous in war, whether it is wealth or victory.... But all these seem to fall under the political community; for it aims not at present advantage but at what is advantageous for life as a whole.... All the communities, then, seem to be parts of the political community.[2]

In this passage, Aristotle sets out what were to become the established elements of civil society—a plurality of associational forms, organized to meet a wide range of common purposes, and collectively subsumed under the aegis of a city's common political life. Two things might be pointed out here: first, the purpose of the political community was to pursue what was deemed to be in the common interest of the *whole* community, not just a part; second, there was no distinction between the formal political state (the polis) and civil society, the political community comprised of its citizens. In short, politics, realized as the pursuit of the common good, is the means by which a community perfects itself. It is the story of how humankind makes life meaningful and fruitful.

It was not until after the Enlightenment that this view of civil society was to change. Like Aristotle, early English political writers made no distinction between state and society (Hooker, Hobbes, Locke). Civil society was political society. For these writers, civil society was a political union based on the consensual arrangement of individuals in a community. Before political union or civil society, there was only the state of nature. John Locke adopted the Aristotelian idea that civil society was a natural product of human sociability (in contrast to Hobbes, who viewed society as a battleground of competing interests). Locke believed that this nature was divinely given and included the impetus to form social groups—a product of natural law: "God having made man such a creature, that in his own judgment, it was not good for him to be alone, put him under strong obligations of necessity, convenience, and inclination to drive him into society."[3]

This vision of human nature also led to Locke's idea that the power of the state was limited to the legitimacy it received from the consent of the governed. Natural law gives men natural rights, discoverable by reason, and where rulers contravene the natural rights of their subjects, they may be overthrown. Thus, Locke acted as a crucial hinge in the evolution of the concept of civil society, incorporating the Aristotelian notion of man as naturally inclined to form communities of common interest, but also distinguishing the common interest and well-being of a community from its institutions of governance. Locke was thus a central figure in establishing the idea of the legitimacy of government and hence, of the autonomous status of the society as a natural community, pre-existing and independent of the forms by which it is governed. Owing largely to Locke, civil society in its modern meaning is thus sharply distinguished from the state and acts as the legitimizing source of the state and of institutional political power.

Along with the rationalist philosophers of the French Enlightenment, major contributions to the idea of civil society were made by the thinkers of the Scottish Enlightenment. These included figures like Adam Ferguson and his friend and colleague, Adam Smith. Ferguson was the first to treat civil society as the subject of a major work. But like his Scottish colleagues, Ferguson rejected the rationalist's metaphysical approach of using abstract theory as the basis for explaining social behavior. He was an empiricist and a cultural pluralist.

"Nations...like private men, have their favourite ends, and their principal pursuits, which diversify their manners, as well as their establishments."[4] For Ferguson, civil society did not arise from purposive decision—some kind of social contract as Rousseau or Hobbes would have it—but as a slow emergence of historical circumstances. Civil society described the culture of a people—it was not a synonym for political society or the state.[5] This distinctive sense of cultural identity has stuck to the term to this day.

The final point I wish to make about the evolution of the term *civil society* is how it relates to the subject of economics. It was Adam Smith who took the idea of "enlightened self-interest," first articulated by Edmund Burke, and postulated it as the famous (infamous?) "invisible hand" that guided the inner workings of society according to its own laws, distinct and apart from those imposed by the state. These rules meant that society could be seen as an independent, integrated whole, which the state should serve. For Smith, as for Burke, the state should be neither the embodiment of society nor its master, but its servant.[6] Moreover, by allowing everyone to follow their own self-interest, the good of all would be served. This is the view developed in *The Wealth of Nations*. But the role of self-interest was only one aspect of Smith's philosophy. He gave equal weight to the notion of "sympathy"—the presence of interpersonal feelings and bonds that make up the relational fabric of civil society.

What happens next is one of those twists in the history of ideas whose impact literally shifts the course of history. Perhaps because it so fitted the values of a now dominant commercial class, Burke's idea of "enlightened self-interest" and Smith's idea of the "invisible hand" were soon interpreted in a manner that subsumed society itself to the particular workings of the market—and the interests of those who controlled it. And whereas in Smith the economy is part of civil society—a particular arrangement of its organizing relationships—it was a sphere of life that was value neutral. There was no place in it for the moral values that underpinned civil life. The idea of the free market soon came to portray the economy as an autonomous, self-regulating sphere of its own. As in the case of a free society, a free market entailed autonomy from the shackles of state rule. Smith's ideas were then pressed into the service of ends that Smith would have abhorred.

Political Economy, Civil Economy, and the Common Good

In Smith's formulation, political economy is a matrix composed of two primary elements, society and the state. This dichotomy has shaped our understanding of the common good. There is, of course, a general notion of the common good as something that benefits the whole of a community, not only a part. But beyond this, there is a more precise definition that distinguishes the *common* good from what economists in the Smithian tradition of political economy usually write about: the *total* good. The distinction is central to our conception of how an economy should function, what its purpose is, and how its benefits are distributed.

If the objective is to maximize the total good, it is immaterial if that also means reducing the good of some individuals, so long as the sum total is increased. Gross domestic product is a formulation of the total good. Inequality does not enter into it. But equality is an essential attribute of the common good. The common good does not allow for the good of one individual to be sacrificed to augment the good of another. The common good, by its nature, is shared equally. Once this principle is violated, it ceases to be the common good.

This conception of the common good was elaborated not in the dichotomous state/society schema of Smith's political economy, but in the Italian tradition of *civil economy* developed by Antonio Genovesi, a contemporary of Smith and a leader of the Italian Enlightenment at the time. Genovesi, an abbot from the town of Salerno, occupied the first Chair of Economics (actually, Chair of *Civil Economy*), which was established at the University of Naples in 1753. He and his followers shared Smith's understanding of the economy as a dimension of civil life. But their goals were different.

Unlike Smith, Genovesi believed that self-interest alone did not allow for the proper functioning of the market. His aim, and what he saw as the purpose of an economy, was public happiness and the full flowering of the human personality—a very Aristotelian ideal.[7] For Genovesi, the common good cannot be achieved without *intentional* benevolence, the practice of *fraternity*. Mutual aid, not merely *mutual advantage* as in Smith's schema, is equally a principle of the economy. In the Smithian tradition, morality and fraternity have no place in the market. The common good is automatically produced as a *non-intentional* by-product of self-interest. The difference in the two paradigms derives from a fundamental difference in their conception of Man and society. This, in turn, is central to the argument set out in the pages that follow.

Smith's formulation of political economy derives from Hobbes's view of Man as a self-interested combatant in a "war of each against all." Genovesi's conception of civil economy derives from a view of Man as a sociable animal flourishing through interpersonal relationships of reciprocity and mutual aid.[8] And, whereas Smith and his followers concerned themselves primarily with the production of wealth, the object pursued by Genovesi and the Neapolitan school was the production of human happiness.

We shall explore this notion of civil economy in greater detail when we consider its relation to the idea of the Partner State in the closing section of the book.

There is a clear sense in which the collection of social attributes we have ascribed to civil society—political autonomy, plurality, common interest, participation in voluntary association—also defines essential elements of democracy itself. In important ways, civil society has now inherited the virtues that were once vested in the political institutions of the liberal nation-state. And this represents a fundamental shift in the dynamics of political legitimacy. It is a seminal moment that reflects the temper of the times. The established forms of representative democracy are leaving citizens feeling powerless, frustrated, and ineffectual, and it is against these that civil power is now being mobilized. But civil power is a sword that cuts two ways.

There is a tendency to read into civil society all the best attributes of an idealized democracy. For many progressives, civil society has become the repository of all that is lacking in the state as we know it. But does this positive image hold up, or is it merely a projection of our own frustrated desires? The Ku Klux Klan is also a (hooded) face of civil society, one we prefer not to look at. The current upsurge of right wing populism is also a product of civil society and forms a counterpoint to the kinds of civil mobilizations that progressives identify with. And if mass marches for civil rights or the environment signify one set of values, populist movements to block immigration or to build border walls or to attack Congress signify something else. What is taking place in the U.S. today is a stark reminder of how civil societies collapse when political institutions are incapable of regenerating fundamental civil values. Ominously for our purposes, entrenched political interests are increasingly aligning themselves around forms of reactionary populism that upend those values of civil society that we have come to embrace as emblematic of democracy itself.

We have reason to worry. And we must look carefully at the assumptions we are making and the hopes we vest in them. For it is in the presumed qualities of civil society that so many hopes for progressive system change have come to rest.

In the opening chapter, we considered the question of how co-operation and the inclination to mutual benefit are hardwired into the human makeup. Selfishness and competitive self-interest are no less prevalent. In many ways, the difference between these two opposing views of human nature is what differentiates the political philosophies of so many of the thinkers we have been discussing. Their political theories range from the gloomy vision of Hobbes, who famously declared that "every man is Enemy to every man," and that human life is "solitary, poor, nasty, brutish, and short," to the felicitous views of Aristotle and Genovesi, for whom co-operation and sociability were defining features of humankind.

What concerns us is the balance of forces that trend the evolution of civil societies toward one disposition as opposed to another. This not to say that co-operation and mutual benefit—the principles of social bonding—are always positive. Fascism is an example of a particular type of co-operation and social bonding. In a provocative challenge to conventional notions of the inherent goodness of civil society, Dylan Riley makes a compelling case that the rise of fascism in Europe was dependent on the existence of vibrant civil societies and the full-blooded support of civil associations.[9] In this analysis, civil society was the source of both the impulse toward democratic freedoms and the impetus to authoritarianism when these freedoms were betrayed by the failure of liberal political institutions to offer a political vision and a vehicle for their realization.

Ironically, both fascism and marxism—at least in its Leninist form—bring us full circle to the old idea that civil society and the institutions of the state are one and the same. They propose that the consummation of human history is to be found in the perfection of the state as a kind of superego. Marx's notion of the withering away of the state ultimately entails the dissolution of civil society (which he sees as a battleground of class exploitation) into a classless, unitary community where politics and power also cease.

On the surface, these notions bear a resemblance to the Aristotelian notion of the city-state as the ultimate expression of human association and sociability. But there is an essential difference. Aristotle saw this as an evolutionary process that proceeded through the practice of politics—the direct engagement of free citizens in running the affairs of their communities. His politics presupposed the possibility of difference, and disagreement. Fascism and Marxism both wish to dispense with politics altogether. And, to a very troubling degree, many of the popular mobilizations we are witnessing today also espouse the same view—that politics does not work, that liberal political institutions are failing, and that the answer may lie in scrapping politics as the means to pursue social change. They are susceptible to the authoritarian impulses of a demonic narcissist like Trump, a butcher like Bolsonaro, or even a buffoonish man-child like Boris Johnson. Meanwhile, profound problems ranging from gross inequality, to economic precarity, to climate catastrophe remain unaddressed.

This disenchantment with politics infects both the left and the right. It is present in the disavowal of representative democracy as much by neo-anarchists extolling "leaderless movements" and the turn to communitarian localism as by the resurrection of the divine right of rulers by evangelicals and the apocalyptic fears of right wing militias arming themselves against the malign schemes of their governments.

In fact, the real issue before us is not that politics has failed but that politics has effectively stopped. It has been on life support for some time. Globalization has rendered politics meaningless because the supranational power of financial and corporate interests has created a scenario in which nation-states are impotent to act in any way that contravenes the interests of these powers. Or, as Zygmund Bauman has put it, "the nation-state is full of politics but increasingly devoid of power."[10] In this scenario, leaders—whether of the left or the right—have no option but to play out the modern state's appointed role as handmaid to capital, to convey whatever remains of the global commons into the hands of those who can turn it into profit, and to manipulate the public in service to these ends. If this means turning a deaf ear to the protests and turning politics into a charade, then so be it.

The crisis today calls on us not to pull the plug on politics but to save it. The failure of liberal democracy to protect the democratic freedoms and values on which its legitimacy rests has generated a desperate search for a new legitimacy, one that responds both to the renewal of democratic values and, through them, to the resolution of unprecedented fears and dangers. Among these, and perhaps the most dangerous of all, is the growing desire for chaos within sectors of the populace whose sympathies lie precisely with those who would burn down the entire edifice that has soured their hopes and betrayed their trust. This is precisely what is unfolding in the U.S. today. The sense of grievance and the thirst for vengeance have fused.

◆　◆　◆

Dylan Riley's account of fascism's rise in the interwar years offers up some timely lessons with respect to politics and the role of the state. Riley documents the explosive growth of civil associations in the late 19th and early 20th centuries, and how these associations were both a product of and catalysts for the formation of democratic political institutions. For many of these associations, the motive force was a demand for more democracy, the creation of a more representative political order than that which buttressed a narrow, privileged sliver of the society.

In Riley's analysis, European fascism emerged from societies in which civic and associational development outstripped the development of the political parties that comprised the existing political order. The traditional parties were unable or unwilling to formulate the kinds of responses that were adequate to the mounting pressures for political reform. Riley rejects analyses that present fascism as a rejection of democracy and instead argues that it can best be understood as a rejection of existing political *institutions*.

Fascism offered new institutions and authoritarian solutions to a crisis of legitimacy. It was a rejection of the procedural aspects of democracy (i.e., voting, competing parties, competing ideologies) and "offered a superior way of connecting the population to the state" through "non-political interest presentation." Fascism provided a more authentic connection between the political regime and the "authentic" will of the people. In what seems like an oxymoron, Riley calls this authoritarian democracy, a representative state *without politics*.

There are serious questions to be raised about a definition of democracy that focuses exclusively on the principle of legitimacy while ignoring its *operational* meaning as a form of participatory politics and effective personal agency. The notion of authoritarian democracy as presented by Riley ignores the *functional* meaning of the word, which is central to our argument and without which democracy becomes a hollow term. However, Riley's account is instructive. It resonates with current conditions in which an ongoing crisis of political legitimacy is being replayed in the rejection of traditional politics by large swathes of the electorate in liberal regimes—especially in Western Europe, the U.K., and the U.S. where populist leaders have arisen to fill a political void.

Like the interwar era, the incapacity of traditional political parties to respond to what Gramsci called the "organic crisis" of the state is being repeated. An organic crisis is a "comprehensive crisis" of the entire political system that, for whatever reason, is no longer able to generate societal consensus (in material or ideological terms). Such a crisis lays bare fundamental contradictions in the system that the ruling elites are unable to resolve. Organic crises are at once economic, political, social, and ideological—in Gramscian terms, they are crises of hegemony—and they lead to a rejection of established political parties, economic policies, and value systems. The signs are everywhere that the liberal political order is undergoing precisely such a crisis. The question for us today is, what will emerge as a response?

If present-day demagogues are able to capitalize on popular discontent, it is because there is little on offer to channel this discontent in more positive directions. Certainly, *audacity*—the willingness to seriously turn things on their heads—is a winning factor. It almost doesn't matter from which direction it is coming, so long as it promises *change*. The parties of the left continue to be paralyzed by fear of giving offence, or of seeming too radical. They are trapped in the frame that has been placed on them by the right. The inability of the left to relate its radical roots to the current context has resulted in the extinction of the parties of the postwar left in most of Europe. In the current crisis, the only places where the left has succeeded is where it has lived up to its historical ideals and fought for convictions that took direct aim at the neoliberal order of the status quo— in Spain and Portugal, and also in Greece, before Syriza betrayed those convictions and abandoned its progressive populism once it was in power.

Therein lie some lessons. Radical principled stands against the status quo can work as easily for the left as for the right, and the failure to articulate a clear alternative hands the game to the forces of reaction who, unlike the disoriented and demoralized left in general, have no qualms about calling out their enemies and waging ruthless battle to realize their aims. It does not hurt them either that the ideology of the time is so suited to their purpose, that they are not bound by the constraints of democracy, and that the power of capital and the institutions of a captured state always line up to ensure their victory.

Meanwhile, the massive eruptions of civil discontent continue, a lava flow of frustration and rage whose direction of travel is both unpredictable and unstoppable.

✦ ✦ ✦

The popular movements of 2011 to 2013 that followed the 2008 financial crisis were in large part a reaction to the crisis of representation in capitalist society. Their response was not mere protest. They were also experiments in the creation of a different democratic model characterized by popular assemblies, horizontal self-organization, and decentralized networks of mutual aid. They adopted novel forms of democratic community and direct democracy in the here and now—not as a demand but as a living practice. Above all, their demand for authentic democracy rejected the ineffectual forms of representation that have neutered electoral politics.

But can this type of mobilization be effective for the kinds of changes being sought? How do "formless" movements acquire the expertise and the systems for sustained reflection and planning that provide political direction and continuity over time? Can such a movement shift from being reactive to a set of particular circumstances to being proactive around a sustained program of change with the power and means to effect it?

It is doubtful. Apart from the power to highlight issues, to express discontent, and even to topple regimes that have lost legitimacy, the creation of durable civil and political institutions is essential if mass mobilizations are to protect the gains they achieve and to transform these gains into systemic changes that last over time. History has shown repeatedly that the absence of this sustaining, institutional capacity leads to defeat and worse.

The case is often made that political movements aiming at this kind of system change require a compelling narrative—a crystallizing story that captures and projects the inner meaning of their struggle. Moreover, it must be a story that can draw in and unite people around a new vision that encompasses the whole of a community's collective life and purpose, what Gramsci called a new hegemony. As argued by Riley, it was the failure of political institutions to create such a hegemony that precipitated the rise of fascism in the interwar period.

In the first decades of the 1800s, the explosive rise of civil associations throughout Europe, including peasant leagues and cooperatives in the countryside and worker organizations and trade unions in the industrial centers, constituted a formidable new force demanding more authentic forms of democracy in government. The role of government as a representative and deliberative body of the people was not at issue. What was at issue was the completion of the democratic project through an extension of its liberal values to include the whole of a society, not merely its governing elites.

This is no longer the case. Liberal democracy itself has been called into question. The contradictions between an ostensibly democratic political system and the inability of elected governments to champion and protect the interests of citizens have discredited representative democracy as a model of governance. The legitimacy of the system is in peril, and the hegemony that has prevailed this past two centuries is no more.

The roots of this crisis of legitimacy are clear. They are expressed directly and loudly in the continuing outbursts of popular discontent from one end of the globe to the other, from both the left *and* the right. The crisis of representation is now present in every major mass mobilization—whether it appears on the streets of the European capitals or in the favelas of the global South. They are a global social response to a historical shift in the relationship between capital and the state on the one hand and the people and representative institutions on the other. What is far from clear is how a political system that depends on the patronage of undemocratic elites can satisfy the calls for radical reform without destroying itself.

The mobilization of civil power mirrors the transformations of capital power and, in a way unprecedented in history, is emerging as a global force to confront not only particular conditions of economic or political injustice but also the far more menacing question of environmental collapse that now threatens the survival of our species. The resistance today, unlike previous eras, is not channeled through parties and established organizations. The foundational issues do not focus merely on questions of material reproduction nor can they be alleviated by tinkering with the system. Rather, they concern the encroachment of inhuman forces into the fabric of everyday life, the hollowing out of human experience, and the extinction of authentic forms of living. As Habermas has remarked, they "concern the grammar of the forms of life."[11]

Driven by the increasingly integrated and global nature of the world economy, civil power has had to contend with larger and larger scales of mobilization. But it is an uneven contest. Capital power is instantly mobile, impersonal, carried in the circuits of global technology and reconstituted through the images and influences of commercial culture. Civil power is physical, present in the assembled bodies of the people, and mobilized with difficulty by concerted and patient effort over time. It is slowed by the inertia and demands of daily living. It requires the accumulation of grievance and the catalyst of common purpose. This common purpose is normally bound by the horizon of what is personal and immediate in one's community or country. Humans live and act at human scales. Capital does not.

If radical change is indeed possible, what does it entail? I would argue that the following are minimal requirements to reverse the tide of economic, social, and environmental damage that is resulting from the collusion of corporate power and the state.

1. Economic democratization—the extension of democratic principles into the economy, at every level.
2. Governmental democratization—the radical restructuring of the state, its purpose, and its operations.
3. Reclamation of the commons—the recovery and protection of commonwealth.
4. Environmental restoration—the reversal of ecological damage.
5. Societal restoration—the rebuilding of mutualism, social trust, and human connection.
6. Humanization of technology—the redesign of technology for social benefit.
7. Global co-operation—the intersection of local autonomy with global accountability.

In the chapters that follow, we will come to terms with some of these issues by looking at specific instances where communities have grappled with these problems and arrived at novel solutions. At the heart of these efforts, there lie the questions of collective action, of the reformative role of civil institutions, and how systems of governance might embody principles of democracy, equality, and the common good. What lessons for system change do these examples offer? And what kind of story needs to be told if the disparate elements striving for a new kind of political economy are to unite behind a common vision and direction for the change we seek? This was present in the forces that ushered in the democratic revolutions of the 17th and 18th centuries; it was present in the uprisings that shook the liberal democracies of the 19th century and culminated in the revolutions of 1848; and it is present now, in embryonic form, in the global call for climate justice and the growing awareness that co-operation and the interdependence of the global human community are fundamental to the democratic promise.

THE COMMONS: DISPOSSESSION AND RECLAMATION

What the poor really need is morals.
— GEORGE GILDER

THE CITY OF CHENNAI is located on the east coast of India, facing out to the Bay of Bengal. With a population of 10 million, Chennai (formerly Madras) is India's sixth most populous city. Along the wide, sandy beach that flanks the city, residents gather among the food stalls and fishing boats to find respite from the stifling heat. The women, ever mindful of Hindu modesty, and draped in stunning explosions of colour, wade sari-clad into the surf. At low tide, just south of the city at Mahabalipuram, visitors can view the traces of sunken stone temples that materialize like ghosts from the depths offshore. Built over 1,200 years ago on what was then the coastline, they are a daily reminder of the deep well of history that haunts the present.

Chennai has always suffered the caprice of its seasons. The monsoon arrives and departs unpredictably. Sometimes it doesn't arrive at all. But on June 19, 2019, following its fourth straight year of record drought, Chennai ran out of water. The event made headlines around the globe, but what was not reported was that 40 percent of India was also facing drought. Six hundred million faced severe water shortages just as a fatal heat wave was sweeping the country. Chennai is now one of 21 cities in India that will run out of groundwater by 2021.[1]

The water crisis in Chennai has been two centuries in the making. It is a case study of dispossession that has led from the careful management of water as a common resource to its commodification and privatization under a neoliberal program financed by the flagship of free market thinking, the World Bank. The privatization of water in Chennai is part of a historical process of dispossession that began with the rise of capitalism in England and has now spread around the globe. The role of the state in this process and the challenges that enclosure poses to the well-being of communities calls for a fundamental reappraisal and reversal of the market doctrines that have led to this crisis in Chennai, and in cities everywhere. The privatization of water is indicative of the global forces that are undermining the fragile balance of the world's ecosystems and the health of communities the world over. The water crisis in Chennai is a wake-up call for change.

In this part of India, water management was the key to balancing the needs of small farmers that relied on irrigation for their crops and the needs of the agrarian settlements. Growth in this region was determined not by the availability of land but of water. Villages in Chennai and the surrounding districts maintained this balance through a system of interlocking commons called *Poramboke* that included vast tracts of land, water bodies, grazing grounds, and woods. Water use was regulated through the building of *erys*, shallow water reservoirs scooped from the earth and connected by canals that supplied the water needs of rural settlements, both for irrigation and domestic use. Construction on these land and water commons was outlawed. The *erys* were not only a method for harvesting and distributing water; their stored water was essential for replenishing groundwater. Agriculture here was entirely dependent on this decentralized water management system and the social organization that sustained it. The co-operative management of vital ecosystems such as commons—in particular, the *erys* system—had sustained this ancient culture for centuries, as it has done for other cultures the world over.[2]

All this changed with the coming of the British.

Madras was the first major English settlement in India. Originally built in 1640, Fort St. George was an outpost of the British East India Company, situated on a small scrap of land six miles long near the fishing village of Madraspatnam. Built to safeguard Britain's trade monopoly in silk and spices against her French and Dutch rivals, the fort soon became a burgeoning trading center. Born as a colony of the British and radiating the attitudes of its colonial masters, Madras quickly colonized the surrounding countryside, setting in motion a pattern of accelerating rapacity and ruin that was to typify British colonial rule for the next three hundred years.

The decline of the rural commons in India reflected the individualistic, aristocratic, and hierarchical mindset of the British overlords and replicated the radical transformations that were taking place half a world away in the shires of England. The eradication of the commons in India, and the intricate ways of communal life that depended on them, was a future foretold by Britain's own history and the particular mindset regarding property that the British imposed on their Indian subjects.

The difference between the British and the Indian concept of property rested on vastly different conceptions of individual rights. In India, property did not reflect ownership but rather a complex of common rights operating on the land. The British did not recognize common forms of property and immediately subsumed village commons into state ownership, with responsibility for their management coming under the control of a Department of Public Works. The first stage of a radical transformation of rural economic and social relations was thus the centralization of power and control from the villages to the state.

The second stage entailed the transformation of cultivated land from a source of sustenance to cultivators and rural communities into a source of revenue for the East India Company, its shareholders in England, and the state. This included the forced adoption of cash crops such as cotton and indigo to replace traditional food cultivation. The third component in this process was the creation of a local landowning nobility such as the one that existed in Britain—the *zamindars*, who, like the landed gentry in Britain, subsisted on the rent extracted from the small cultivators who worked the land.

The creation of a subject class subservient to a propertied nobility, which was in turn controlled by British colonial officers, was central to British imperialism. The total effect was the destruction of those reciprocal social relations that sustained common systems of survival—water management being key among them—and the dispossession, pauperization, and dependence that this produced. The destruction of the commons in South India was dispossession of the population from both the social and material basis of their survival.

Of course, India was not alone in this process. The capitalist system that evolved in England depended on the colonization and dispossession of peoples and places the world over. The money that fuelled capitalism came from the slave trade in Africa and the silver and gold that was shipped to Europe from the conquered territories and slave mines of the New World.

The parallels in colonial India with the destruction of the English peasantry and the enclosure of the commons during the industrialization of England are clear. So, too, are the links to the current crisis of the state and the provision of essential services to citizens—not only in the U.K. but worldwide. The erasure of the commons and the co-operative systems and values that sustained them is at the heart of this story.

A *common* may be defined as any resource that is shared by a community of users along with the social relationships or rules that govern that use. As David Bollier, has put it, commons "are more accurately defined as paradigms that combine a distinct community with a set of social practices, values and norms that are used to manage a resource. Put another way, a common is a resource + a community + a set of social protocols." The three are key elements of an integrated whole.[3]

As in the case of the *Poramboke* and the *erys* system in India, a common could be water rights, pastures, forests, and even the infrastructure such as tanks and canals that are collectively managed for a community of users. The common is shared co-operatively according to rules accepted by that community and is managed jointly by them. These use rights, and the ways they are enforced, vary widely from one place to another. But commoning, however varied, entails far more than *mere use* of the resource.

The common is bound up in a dense network of reciprocal relationships that constitutes a social substratum of co-operation and mutual aid on which the common rests. Without this substratum, the common could not subsist. It is the social relationships and the communal recognition of individual rights and obligations, as well as collective responsibilities, that maintain the common. In turn, the destruction of a common also destroys the co-operative social relations and attitudes that sustained it. For a small community, the loss of a common has profound effects on the dense fabric of social connections that are woven into a system of sharing that draws from, and reinforces, co-operation as an essential social good.

Until quite recently, Britain was a land in which commons were the foundation of the rural economy and covered almost the whole of England and Scotland. The disappearance of almost all this commonwealth of land took about three centuries, from the 1500s to the 1800s.

In Britain today, 25,000 landowners—0.06 percent of the population—owns 50 percent of the land.[4] Thirty percent is owned by the aristocracy and gentry, which has remained ensconced on its estates for centuries. Eighteen percent is owned by corporations. A further 17 percent is owned by oligarchs of varying types—bankers, businessmen, politicians, etc. Independent homeowners own a mere 5 percent of the land, and with the current skyrocketing value of real estate, this figure is shrinking. Conservation charities, like the National Trust, own a paltry 2 percent. The largest corporate landowner is United Utilities, a water company.

These figures show, in the clearest possible way, the gross inequities of the country and dispel any notions that class, and the privileges of the British aristocracy, have diminished in any way. The British elites remain as tenacious as barnacles on the hide of history. Their accumulation of wealth and power, of which their landholdings are the most visible display, are the product of the centuries-long process of dispossession and capital accumulation that established the material basis of capitalism and its current phase of universal growth through globalization. It has taken 500 years of steady plunder to accomplish this end.

The inequality that is baked into capitalism fosters discontent and defiance. But it also inoculates elites against the sufferings of their victims. In 2014, a fascinating experiment was conducted at the UC Berkeley campus to gauge the psychological effects of privilege. In this experiment, pairs of randomly selected subjects flipped a coin before playing a game of Monopoly. The winner of the coin toss received certain advantages over their opponent. They started off with more money and could roll two dice to their opponent's one. In this way, the game was rigged to ensure that they would win. Within moments of starting the game, the "rich" players became more dominant, more aggressive in their play, and showed less consideration for their opponent. They became ruder. They even consumed more of the snacks provided by the researchers. When asked why they won, "rich" players cited factors like their own good judgement or strategic play. Not a single one answered that it was because of the advantages they had won from a random coin toss.[5]

Privilege influences the behavior and attitude of individuals regardless of their background or political outlook. In a wonderfully even-handed way, privilege produces crappier people, regardless of their background. This goes a long way to explaining the indifference of elites to the broader social consequences of their privilege. Personal merit is bestowed as a *consequence* of wealth, not as a cause of it. The wealthier you are, the more entitled to that wealth you are likely to feel. In turn, this entitlement is passed on through the mythology of family and class exceptionalism and the class replicators of elite schools, corporate placements, and political sinecures.

Over the course of this history, enclosure has been the most effective method of removing common lands from collective ownership and handing it to private individuals. And, as was the case in

India, the justification for privatizing the land was the same: to improve its efficiency and to maximize its economic value. Ideology and self-interest have always factored into these arguments. The central element in this worldview is the idea of isolated individuals who operate alone, outside any social framework for managing co-operation, and whose sole interest is personal gain regardless of the social cost. This is what contemporary economics defines as "rational"—a caricature of the capitalist individual driven solely by self-interest—the sociopathic *homo economicus* of neoliberal lore.

Today, the issue of enclosure has global implications. They include the management of global commons in an era of environmental defilement, the privatization of public wealth, the disappearance of cultural diversity, and the conflict between globalism and the survival of the local.

The birth of this fictional *homo economicus* that is at the center of the neoliberal worldview was a forced labor that took centuries. It evolved alongside the destruction of the social relations that sustained a very different conception of man and society. Co-operation, mutual aid, and the commons were the social matrix of this older worldview, now entirely lost from sight. The world of the commons, and the peasant social ecology that it sustained, did not go without a struggle—a battle over values and worldviews that continues, with increasing urgency, to this day.

The idea that private rights to property supersede those of common usage is an entirely modern notion. In England, where the idea of absolute rights over private property first appeared, common usage of land by peasants was established practice. The entire cycle of peasant life, from access to the life-sustaining resources of fields, forests, fens, and waterways, to the ways in which the land itself was cultivated, depended on interlocking systems of co-operation, commons, and mutual aid that sustained the rural community along with the entire edifice of feudal society that rested upon it. Commons were the social and material bedrock of peasant existence.

Enclosure became the pivotal issue for the future of agriculture in Britain. It pitted the values and life patterns of a common rights economy against the interests of a rising class of wealthy landowners, with commoners confronting proto capitalists. Capitalism, it should be remembered, did not begin in the towns and cities. Mass urbanization was its effect. Capitalism began in the countryside with the radical transformation of social and economic relations in the old agricultural economy. The basis of these transformations was the domestication of the peasantry.

What began in the Middle Ages as a naked attempt by landowners to appropriate common resources for themselves, evolved in the 1700s and 1800s into a campaign to drive peasants off the land by depriving them of their livelihood. The aim—stated clearly and unequivocally—was to transform independent farmers and artisans into wage laborers, an agrarian proletariat. By eliminating the commons, the foundation of a self-sustaining and independent existence for small cultivators was knocked from beneath their feet. Dispossession was imperative for the proletarianization of the peasantry and a precondition for the transition from agricultural to industrial capitalism.

During this entire process, the state, under the firm control of the aristocracy and the rising bourgeoisie, acted as handmaid to the interests of the upper class. Between 1760 and 1870, seven million acres of common land were enclosed through the enactment of 4,000 separate acts of parliament. This was equivalent to one-sixth the area of England.[6] The need for cheap labor and a proletarian class that worked for wages could not coexist with a common rights economy or the peasant independence that it made possible. Independence and freedom were only for the deserving rich. Deserving rich require the existence of undeserving poor. The arguments that were used to justify the exploitation of the poor are resurrected with unfailing predictability to justify class malice to this day. The very term *commoner* took on the unshakeable stigma of crudeness and low class that it bears still.

Apologists for the immiseration of the peasantry were quite clear in their motives, and their prescriptions went far beyond mere dispossession. Nearly all of the big names in early political economy agreed on the need for discipline and enforced labor on the poor.

Francis Hutcheson, the teacher of Adam Smith, declared: "If a people have not acquired an habit of industry, the cheapness of all the necessaries of life encourages sloth. The best remedy is to raise the demand for all necessaries.... Sloth should be punished by temporary servitude at least."[7]

Here begins the justification for robbing the poor of leisure and ensuring that toil alone should be their lot. But servitude requires a servile mentality. It was one of the chief arguments against the provision of universal education. Without the habituation to perpetual labor of a domesticated class, how else would society support the more worthy in "Idleness, Ease, and Pleasure"?

In his notorious essay on the origin of moral virtue, Bernard Mandeville reflected on the desirability of educating the working poor:

> To make the Society Happy and People Easy under the meanest Circumstances, it is requisite that great numbers of them should be Ignorant as well as Poor. Knowledge both enlarges and multiplies our Desires.... The Welfare and Felicity therefore of every State and Kingdom require that the Knowledge of the Working Poor should be confin'd within the Verge of their Occupations and never extended (as to things visible) beyond what relates to their Calling. The more a Shepherd, a Plowman or any other Peasant knows of the World, and the things that are foreign to his Labor or Employment, the less fit he'll be to go through the Fatigues and Hardships of it with Chearfulness and Content.[8,9]

One could go on indefinitely with such examples of moral superiority comingled with crass self-interest. They all culminate at the same sad place...the justification for a subject class, a subhuman species, a reserve humanity maintained at the lowest possible cost for the production of the highest possible profit. The creation of a dependent working class, contrary to all the professed ideals of a free market, required brutal force, the erasure of a social conscience, and the full weight of the state to achieve. No one gives up their livelihood or liberty willingly. The destruction of the commons and the co-operative ways of living that they made possible was not born of some natural evolution of the market. It was an act of brute compulsion and social engineering on an epic scale. Its effects on the quality of life of the peasantry were incalculable.

The destruction of the commons in England resulted in the reorganization of a rural agricultural society that subsisted on common use rights that sustained a large percentage of smallholders, cottagers, artisans, and landless poor. This changed the composition of rural society into a division of large landowners extracting rack rents from previously enclosed commons, a diminishing number of small farmers, and a growing underclass of landless tenants and laborers. It was this model of society, based on the exclusive and absolute rights of private property and vested in a landed nobility and class privilege, that was exported to the British colonies.

◆ ◆ ◆

The triumph of industrial capitalism in the 19th century was predicated on the extermination of ways of life based on the primacy of social values over the prerogatives of capital and the profit motive. This was The Great Transformation that Karl Polanyi identified—the break between a past in which economic relations were embedded in the norms and values of a pre-existing social order and the emergence of a market society in which capital was divorced from all social control and to whose needs all social values were subsumed. This cleavage was the ultimate meaning of the Industrial Revolution. But what also arose in this period were new forms of commoning, of co-operation and political action that rose up to meet the inhuman conditions created by a wholly alien capitalist reality. The popular mobilization for democracy—which at that time meant outright revolution—was a direct consequence of this radical shift in economic and social relations.

In Great Britain, the co-operative movement that took form at this time extended and adapted the mutualist values that had underpinned the common rights economies of the countryside. It sought to create new forms of co-operative organization to challenge industrial capitalism—both as a form of economic organization and as a vision of human society. Co-operativism at the start of the 19th century was but one branch of a universal movement for social reform that included the demand for universal suffrage, the rise of trade unions, the demand for women's rights, and the attempt to preserve the values of craftsmanship and labor's control over work against the onslaught of the machine age.

All of this was part of the tremendous explosion of associationism, of the emergence of autonomous voluntary groupings, which became the seedbed of modern civil society. The rise of civil society was a consequence of many factors—economic disruption, radical mobilization, and the freedoms that ensued from the liberalization of political space. In every case, the shape and character of civil society were to play a pivotal shape in the political trajectory of the state, in the clash of contending interests, and in the constitution of the society as a democratic polity.

If the disappearance of the commons marked the end of an economic system based on communal rights and social interdependence, the co-operative movement was a monumental effort to recast these values for an industrial age. The movement's influence spread rapidly, generating co-operatives of all types across Europe, Russia, and the Ukraine. From Britain, the co-op idea was carried to North America on the waves of emigration that followed the enclosures, famines, and rural depopulation of the mid-1800s. Co-operatives were to play a signal role in the lives of working people both in the New World and the old.

Today, co-operatives represent the foremost example of economic democracy and the most significant working alternative to the capitalist model. They are not merely a relic of a bygone era. There are over 3 million co-operatives, and globally they employ over 280 million people; the livelihoods of over 10 percent of the world's population depend either directly or indirectly on co-operatives.[10] In basic sectors of the economy, from agriculture and fishing, to financial services, to social care and housing, co-ops sustain the well-being of millions of people and provide essential social and economic services to communities at the furthest reaches of the globe. They remain a constant reminder that there are other, more humane ways of understanding and practicing economics in the service of social values. Their significance as the linchpins to system change and the recovery of co-operative social values will be explored in detail in the coming chapters.

The New Enclosures

In Britain, the battle for the survival of social and co-operative values in the economy rages still. But dispossession and enclosure have taken new forms. In the past, commons were embodied in the economies and social relations of the countryside. In the postwar era, a large part of the commons was now composed of the public wealth that had been built up with the emergence of the welfare state. This included the hospitals, schools and universities, libraries, railways, roads, ports and harbors, fire brigades, telecommunications systems, postal systems, and public parks—the whole spectrum of social goods that were paid for by taxes and the labor of the populace. It was this assemblage of services, resources, and public institutions that composed the public commonwealth of the nation.

With the election of Margaret Thatcher in 1982, all of this came under threat. New forms of enclosure and privatization were proposed using the same rationale that was employed to enclose the commons of an earlier era. Privatization would make these public industries and services—the public commonwealth—more productive according to the commercial logic of profitability. Market logic demanded that anything that could not sustain itself on a profit basis should be closed down or sold off. That the state might provide a social good independently of the profit principle, paid for by taxation and managed as a common asset for the citizenry, was inadmissible. It contravened the notion that only a capitalist market organized solely for the promotion of private profit was legitimate.

Since Thatcher's assault on public wealth in the early 80s, the pace of privatization has accelerated and gone global. By the end of that decade, sales of state enterprises worldwide had reached a total of over $185 billion. In 1990 alone, the world's governments sold off $25 billion in state-owned enterprises—with countries vying to see who could claim the privatization crown. Unsurprisingly, the largest single sale occurred in Britain, where investors paid over $10 billion for 12 regional electricity companies. New Zealand sold more than 7 state-owned companies, including the government's telecommunications company and printing office, for a price that topped $3 billion.[11]

In the U.K., the privatizations that took place under both Tory and Labour governments, along with the tax cuts that accompanied them, represents the single largest transfer of wealth from the public to the private sector in history. What began as a sell-off of poorly performing nationalized industries, primarily in the resource and manufacturing sectors, soon expanded to include basic utilities such as power, telecommunications, transportation, sanitation, and water.

The rush to privatization is not only a result of ideology. It is also because there is so little scope for profitable investment in the private sector. In these volatile times, investment in productive business entails high levels of risk. Business ventures can fail. The financialization of the global economy, coupled with tax breaks and the use of tax havens by the rich, has resulted in a glut of hoarded capital. Globally, there are trillions of dollars in corporate coffers looking for profitable investments. In 2017, American Fortune 500 corporations alone were holding on to $2.6 trillion in offshore tax havens. In Britain, £750 billion are sitting idle, and the wealth hoarded by individuals is up to $36 trillion.[12]

The plunder of public wealth for profit is thus a prime target since all the risk is borne by the taxpayer who will ultimately bail out investors should companies fail. Meanwhile, the cost of privatized services will rise just as certainly as their quality and accessibility will decline. This is particularly disastrous in the case of essential, life-sustaining, non-optional resources.

Such as water.

When Thatcher privatized water services in England and Wales in 1989, the British public was told that the sell-off would increase efficiency, widen share ownership, and generate investment. Instead, the opposite happened. Now, three decades after water was sold off, share ownership is in the hands of a small group of international investors, many of them based in tax havens.

Since privatization, water prices have increased by 43 percent. By comparison, publicly owned Scottish Water provided water services to Scottish customers at a cost that is 2 percent lower than what it was in 2000.[13] Similarly, a comprehensive study of water services in France, where three-quarters of the water supply is delivered by the private sector, found that in 2004 the price of water provided by private companies was 16.6 percent higher than in places where municipalities provided it.[14]

Despite such findings, and the continuing cost to consumers and the public purse not only in water but also in energy, transportation, communications, and a host of other essential services, privatization continues to be promoted by institutions like the World Bank, the IMF, the G20, the OECD, the EU, and international Development Banks. Privitization is worked into the global trade deals that shape the investment and development trajectories of national governments and the global economy. The privatization of vital public institutions across the globe is being fuelled by the financing of public-private-partnerships with trillions of dollars of untapped capital held by pension funds, insurance companies, and institutional investors.

The corporate enclosure of global water commons is certainly among the most malign threats to public welfare being faced today. Global warming is turning water into the most prized—and politically charged—resource on the planet. And if the dispossession induced by the enclosure of common land characterized the first phase of capitalist accumulation in England, the global enclosure of water marks the final act in the inexorable movement of capital to commodify every vestige of life-sustaining resources in the natural world. In an age of global warming and growing deprivation, this is an assault against human well-being and security that is unprecedented. But it is precisely where maximum profits might be made. In a world that's broiling, control over water is the ultimate market leverage.

The process of enclosure and dispossession is never-ending. It is a primary mechanism of capital accumulation, whether we are speaking of the termination of the communal pastures of England or the colonization of the public domain, which now facilitates the plunder of public wealth everywhere. This includes everything in the natural world around us, the public goods and benefits created by our social institutions, and more insidiously still, the appropriation of the immaterial potential of the human mind and personality— in knowledge, in information, in social relations, in the untapped motivations, desires, fears, and fantasies of our individual minds. Surveillance capitalism, mining the incipient possibilities of an age fuelled by information, is the frontline of economic exploitation that now faces us. It is perhaps the final unbridled frontier of a capitalist dystopia that is only now coming into frightening focus.

◆　◆　◆

In Chennai, the water crisis only deepens. For millions of families, the hunt for water dominates the day with people lining up for six hours or more—three in the morning, three in the evening—to receive water. It's a full-time occupation burdening mostly the women, who wait with a kind of ageless weariness, baking in the heat, bearing the brightly coloured plastic water pots that have become a symbol of this spreading calamity. Some line up at wells, some line up at water taps. At the wells, local officials run a lottery to determine who gets to the front of the queue. The lucky first-comers get clear fresh water. The unlucky ones at the end of the line get a mud-coloured liquid.[15]

The privatization of Chennai's water supply was a slow stealth movement of "reform" that began in 1978, with financing and direction from the World Bank. Metrowater was transformed from a public resource to a commercial enterprise organized for profit. By the late 1990s, the model had become dogma for remaking the water sector throughout India. As with the privatized water systems in England and France, the damage to the public interest carried far beyond deficiencies in service. They entailed major environmental costs. Under the new policy, the water utility, responding to customer demand and the drive to maximize revenues, abandoned its duty to protect the region's groundwater resources. Metrowater became the worst offender in depleting the aquifers of the city. It was a central cause of the water shortages that hit crisis levels in 2019.

Water in India, as everywhere else, is not perceived as a mere commodity. It carries a highly symbolic meaning that is sustained by a thick nexus of social and religious practice enacted through complex rituals of gifting, sharing, and rule. As a common, water use embodies an entire galaxy of interpersonal rights and obligations. Until recently, the state has been a repository and steward of these rights. In India, and around the world, a central aspect of the "water wars" that are now raging is "the paradigm war"—how water is perceived, valued, and treated. As Vandana Shiva put it, "The culture of commodification is at war with diverse cultures of sharing, of receiving and giving water as a free gift."[16]

Water, for obvious reasons, strikes a particularly sensitive chord. But by the beginning of the 2000s, the headlong rush to privatization had reached a global high point. Every major sector of the public commonwealth of more than 130 countries had divested or turned over to private management at least 75,000 small and medium enterprises previously owned by the state. The World Bank, among the world's most avid promoters of privatization, is hardly likely to recommend a radical change in direction. In the U.K., calls for taking water back into public ownership are growing. Even Boris Johnson can feel heat from the public mood and renationalized sections of the British rail system. It is not surprising.

But is this the answer? Was it not governments, after all, that privatized formerly public resources, like water? Like energy systems? Like the endless stream of public resources that have been put out to the private sector? Perhaps it is time to think of something beyond this endless seesaw of public versus private ownership? Clearly, neither alternative, on its own, can guarantee protection of the public interest. Perhaps we need to look at something more fundamental—to those values and principles that actually embody the commitment to mutuality, to the effective management of collective goods, to the rebirth of our commonwealth, and to an understanding that individual self-interest and the profit motive are utterly incompatible with the protection of resources essential to the public welfare.

A return to the principles of co-operation and the commons and the capacity to collectively enact these principles through new social and political institutions seem essential for a progressive pathway forward. What might these institutions look like and what are the respective roles of government and civil society in bringing them about? The case studies that follow provide us with examples from which we can learn.

4

THE CO-OPERATIVE CITY

It's not a crisis, I just don't love you anymore.
— Protest sign

WHEN THE FINANCIAL CRISIS hit in 2008, many saw it as a turning point, the final act of a failed system and the ideology that sustained it. Few would have guessed not only that the system would survive but that governments would double down, accelerate the very policies that brought on the calamity, and seek restitution not from its perpetrators but from its victims. The austerity policies that were forced upon the populations of Europe to pay for the bank bailouts bit the most vulnerable economies of the south the hardest—Spain, Portugal, Greece.

In Spain, popular reaction to austerity and disgust at the corruption of the political establishment erupted in 2011, and gave voice to a new sensibility regarding politics and civil power. The civil uprisings in Spain combined the demand for direct democracy with a set of values that reimagined governance and politics from the vantage point of civil power as a central component of what is now recognized as a new municipalism. The case of Spain is extraordinarily illustrative. Spain's experience of translating the precepts of direct democracy and popular mobilization into political power and public policy at the level of the city holds important lessons for our consideration of politics as the interaction of civil power and the institutions of governance.

Spain is a land of extremes. From the incendiary passions of flamenco and the harrowing works of Goya to the sublime vision in stone and stained glass that aspires to heaven in Gaudí's Sagrada Família cathedral in Barcelona, art and culture portray a nation at war with itself. One is reminded of Dali's surrealist painting depicting a huge human form, its face exulting in a horrific grimace as it pulls itself to pieces.[1] The painting was a prophetic premonition of the impending horrors of the Spanish Civil War. "Throughout history," writes Manuel Castells, "politics in Spain has been run ragged by dramas, shocks, and civil wars."[2] Spain is also a land of shifting frontiers—geographical, political, and psychological. Always, it feels as if something immense, as yet unformed, is struggling to be born.

The most recent of the European nations to emerge from its long dictatorship, the fascist era that followed the Spanish Civil War continues to cast its shadow. It was 1936 when a prim, pear-shaped figure, standing at 5'3" and sporting a Hitler moustache, initiated a coup and set fire to a nation. Franco's brutal regime, a blend of fanatical nationalism, authoritarianism, vitriolic anti-communism, and Catholicism, lasted thirty-six long years and ended only with the dictator's death in 1975. The Spanish Civil War has been described as a dress rehearsal for WWII. Understandably so. The fascist atrocities that took place in Spain were a foretaste of what was to follow in the rest of Europe. Estimates of the dead range from 300,000 to one million. No one knows for certain. To this day, the collective trauma of the fratricide remains buried, the wounds unhealed, the demons unexorcised. Spain is a nation awaiting confession to its own conscience.

The protests of the May 15, 2011 movement that followed the global financial crisis and the political sensibility that they expressed cannot be understood without reference to this bloody backdrop. Despite the transition to democracy, the political parties that wielded power after Franco formed a governing elite deeply compromised by corruption. On the surface, parliamentary democracy embodied the usual rights of suffrage and representation. In practice, power alternated between Conservatives and Social Democrats in a two-party system that divided the spoils of corruption with admirable equity. As with PASOK in Greece and the Italian Socialist Party (PSI) in Italy, social democracy in Spain was corrupted by the spoils of power that, in turn, depended on complicity with the interests of capital. It was not only the political culture of Spain that suffered. Its economy remained among the most backward in Europe.

When the financial crisis struck, Spain was hit with particular force. Its banks had invested heavily in the housing bubble, which burst in 2009. As the banks teetered on collapse, the situation became surreal when Socialist Prime Minister Rodríguez Zapatero denied there was any crisis at all and then accepted a €100 billion loan from the European Central Bank and imposed the austerity measures that became the hallmark of EU policy. The Social Democrats then colluded with the right to embed austerity provisions in the constitution. Banks were bailed out, public services were slashed, taxes ballooned, unemployment went ballistic, and the public mood began to simmer.

The boiling point was reached on May 15, 2011 (15-M). On that day, 150,000 citizens responded to a call for action and flooded the streets of 60 towns and cities in Spain. A largely spontaneous movement, the nationwide action was the culmination of a series of protests that had been gathering force across a broad front consisting of some 200 groups operating outside the major unions and political parties. The massive outpouring of 15-M was in response to a call from the internet group Real Democracy Now! that had become a focal point for the protests. The manifesto that was published on the website was not merely a rejection of austerity. It was a rallying cry against the economic and political system and a dysfunctional democracy that no longer represented the people. The broad appeal of this call cut across party lines and social classes and struck a deep chord that resonated with old and young alike. A national poll taken by the *El Pais* newspaper on June 26, revealed that 79 percent of the population backed the movement's demands.

Deeply influenced by the Arab Spring uprisings of the preceding months, the organizers of the 15-M movement took inspiration both from the methods and the meaning of those momentous demands for democracy that spread like holy fire across the Middle East. Like them, the Spanish mobilization relied on the power of online organizing, the catalytic role of social networks, and the physical occupation of public space.

Following the demonstrations on May 15, a small group of 100 protestors decided to occupy la Plaza del Sol, the main square in Madrid. They put up tents, rolled out sleeping bags, set up folding chairs, and settled in for the long haul. In the early hours of the morning, the police descended. They swung truncheons and broke heads and expelled the protestors in a fury of violence. When the news and images of the police actions reached the populace, it was like a dam breaking. Thousands of protestors returned to reoccupy the square, and in the days following, something like a liberation camp was established with between 5,000 and 50,000 occupying the square at any given time. The media began to describe the site as "the republic of Sol." Within a few days of the Madrid occupation, the main squares of 20 cities had been occupied.

But the 15-M movement aspired to more than mere protest. It sought a revolution in how politics was understood and practiced. It aimed for a new kind of politics in the workings of the movement itself. The manner in which the occupations were organized, the sense of community that was fostered, and the way the movement presented itself to the world expressed a clear set of values—a utopia made visible. Above all, the movement aspired to reclaim the "right to the city" for its citizens and to wrest control from the handful of politicians, technocrats, and corporate interests that determined how the city was organized and for whose benefit.

From the start, the movement displayed the influence of anarchist ideas, which had played such a central role in Spain's history. At the start of the Civil War, anarchist groupings formed the core of the Republican resistance to Franco and anarcho-syndicalism had a profound influence on the organization of the Spanish left. These ideas found a new form in the 15-M movement. Decisions were made through deliberations in public assemblies that sometimes numbered in the thousands. Hierarchical positions of leadership were rejected. There were no official spokespersons. There were no affiliations with political parties. The dozens of organizations that came together in this mass movement retained their individuality and autonomy. Mutual aid groups and volunteers supplied the encampments with food, communication systems, toilets, first-aid services, childcare centers, libraries, and legal aid. Each of the camps in the various cities was autonomous; there was no central organizing body co-ordinating their activities. Co-operation was voluntary and self-directed.

The 15-M movement was a radical experiment in direct democracy. The encampments were intended to create, in real life, a model of community envisaged by its advocates. For many, it was a first electrifying exposure to the ideas and practice of co-operative self-governance. They were to become a common standard for the many mass movements that were to follow.

Among the movements that came together under the umbrella of 15-M, the Platform for People Affected by Mortgages (PAH) is worth highlighting, both for its role in the mobilizations and for its leadership. PAH spearheaded the resistance to evictions, the protection of immigrants, and the demand for social justice in housing. Spain's housing crisis exposed the systemic injustices of the country. Encumbered by escalating debt, rising unemployment, and the austerity cuts in wages and benefits, Spanish homeowners soon found they could not afford their mortgage payments. Banks were quick to foreclose, and in the five-year period between 2007 and 2013, over 420,000 foreclosures and 220,000 evictions had occurred.[3]

By physically blocking access to properties facing foreclosure and by negotiating with the banks to reduce homeowners' debt, PAH prevented more than 1,600 evictions and rehoused over 2,500 people, often in empty buildings that it had occupied. What also made PAH unique was its ability to galvanize awareness and support from people that were outside the usual ambit of the activist left. With

actions that were reminiscent of the community organizing strategies of Saul Alinsky in the U.S. during the 60s,[4] it educated, trained,
and mobilized the actual victims of the country's predatory housing and banking policies. PAH's actions were direct, dramatic, and
often laced with humour. When IKEA came out with the catchy
advertising slogan "The independent republic of your home," PAH
took them at their word. They occupied IKEA and slept in the beds.
Unlike IKEA's vacuous marketing speak, PAH's slogan was rather
more caustic: "You'll never have a house in your whole f'king life."

The 15-M movement soon became the source of profound change
in the political map of Spain. But by 2012–2013, the movement had
begun to lose momentum with its focus on occupying the main
plazas. It is not possible to sustain a fever-pitch level of popular mobilization forever. Eventually, people return to their everyday lives.
The challenge facing the movement was how to translate the shift in
political consciousness and the experience of mass mobilization into
something that could be sustained over time. It shifted focus and
began a strategy of dispersing its political action to the neighborhoods. Here, the assemblies were revived, and so began a process of
linking the broader political crisis with the particular issues and concerns of life at the local level. Modeled after the assembly discussions
of the plazas, the neighborhood assemblies engaged residents in a
process of identifying common concerns, deliberating on solutions,
and organizing mutual aid actions.

Most important of all, the process established relationships of
trust between activists and the people most affected by austerity and
the wider inequities of the system. Immigrants and many in the most
vulnerable sectors of society were gradually mobilized and brought
into the broader political arena. Questions of political representation, corruption, and legitimacy were no longer mere abstractions.
They were visible in the very real effects of losing one's home and
a lifetime of debt. This linkage of political principles with concrete
issues of daily survival had enormous consequences for the shifts
that were soon to take place inside Spain's political establishment.

PAH was at the forefront of this process. The organization had established 240 nodes across Spain, with each unit remaining autonomous but actively networking and collaborating with the others. The resistance to evictions and the support offered to their victims established a new political alliance that was rooted in grassroots action focused on real issues that could be addressed at neighborhood level. The process radicalized and empowered thousands who, absent the organizing impetus of PAH and the sense of common bond that it established, would have remained isolated and helpless before the onslaught of the system. The organizing tactics of PAH, and their mobilizing power, were crucial to PAH's popularity and success. Another factor was the central role played by Ada Colau, a leading activist in the organization. Her catalytic power as the voice and image of the movement was a key factor in its popular appeal.

Colau has always been reticent to call herself a leader. She insists on her role being more of a "figurehead" for the movement, something that might be filled by any number of other individuals. This reflects the movement's rejection of hierarchy and authority figures as a matter of principle. But while the rejection of traditional forms of representation may be workable at small scale and over short periods of time, it becomes problematic when matters of sustained political practice, the application of policy, and the organization of effective political power become paramount. It is always this transition from popular movement to political institution that is most problematic for grassroots mobilizations. It is also the issue that is potentially the most divisive for a movement founded on self-organization, direct democracy, and rejection of hierarchy.

The true impact of the 15-M movement became evident in the municipal and regional elections of May 2015. In Barcelona, Ada Colau ran for political office at the head of Barcelona en Comu (Barcelona in Common), a coalition of groups that had arisen from 15-M and the community assemblies. The name was well chosen. It combined the notion of a mobilized public and the idea of the commons to frame a vision of participatory politics that extended well beyond traditional political institutions. The formation of the organization's platform was itself an exercise in participatory democracy. In

September 2014, the organization began a process of citizen consultation in a series of neighborhood assemblies to hammer out a political platform and to establish a Code of Political Ethics.

The principles of the platform were:
+ To guarantee basic social rights and a dignified life for all people
+ To promote an economy with social and environmental justice
+ To democratize institutions and decide on the city we want
+ To assume an ethical commitment with citizens

The Code of Ethics included:
+ Democratization of political representation, control and accountability
+ Financing, transparency, and cost management
+ Professionalization of politics and removal of privileges
+ Measures against corruption

This last provision also included the introduction of a salary cap of 2,200 euros monthly for members of En Comu.

In addition, the platform included a "shock plan" based on the idea of "common and economic viability" to "counter the dehumanization" of austerity policies and to "restore the dignity" of the poorest people.

The completed platform, the forward propulsion of the neighborhood assemblies, and the charismatic role of Ada Colau as the face of the party resulted in the capture of a majority in Barcelona's municipal council. The coalitions of the 15-M movement found themselves governing in all the major cities and regions of Spain and, with the exception of Madrid, Galicia, and Castilla-Leon, wiped away the political base of the People's Party—Spain's foremost conservative party with its roots in the Franco regime. In a mere four years following the mass mobilizations of 15-M, these elections put an end to the two-party system in Spain. 15-M gave the crisis of legitimacy focus and expression. The result was not only a reform tide sweeping across the municipal sector but also a transformation of the left in Spain. The voice of radicalism no longer emanated from the mouths of party politicians but resounded through the streets and in the manifestos of a mobilized citizenry. Could such a voice remain true to its purpose also in the halls of power?

Barcelona en Comu was not interested in contesting the elections as a gesture of protest. They were campaigning to win power and to govern. In so doing, they had to reconcile two very different, and often conflicting, political sensibilities—that of a grassroots movement deeply suspicious of formal politics and the demands of a governing political institution in the making. The contrasting forces were visible when Ada Colau stepped to the microphone in her campaign office to accept her victory as mayor, surrounded by a press of youthful activists dressed in jeans and T-shirts and looking like they just came from a street meeting. The atmosphere was joyous, bordering on delirium, as activist leaders across Spain were swept to power on a tide of outrage and hope. Was it a new dawn or a mere twist of luck?

Economic democracy was a central pillar of En Comu's philosophy. The party sought to expand the role of that sector of the economy that focused on the production of goods and services for people as opposed to profit—the social economy.[5] Often described as the "third sector" alongside the public sector and the private market, the social economy is comprised of those organizations that are driven by their social mission and whose animating principle is reciprocity for mutual benefit. Barcelona en Comu saw the social economy as a transformative sector. The Impetus Plan for the Social and Solidarity Economy put it this way:

> The SSE tries to recover the original function of the economy, putting it at the service of people in order to manage resources equitably and exploit them in a sustainable way, and creating a production model that converts work into an instrument geared towards satisfying people's needs.[6]

Barcelona en Comu saw the social economy as a partner in the co-design of policies that could transform the socioeconomic model of the city. The aim was not only to create services for people but to strengthen the productive capacity of the social economy. The City expanded access to resources, training, public procurement, financing, and the institutional development of the social economy as a whole.

Barcelona's social economy is extensive. It is home to 4,800 socio-economic initiatives, which include 2,400 social enterprises, 1,197 worker-owned enterprises, and 861 co-operatives. The sector employs over 53,000 people and has over 100,000 volunteers. The consumer co-operatives have some 550,000 members, and worker co-ops comprise over 25 percent of the sector's organizations. The Impetus Plan aimed at consolidating and elevating the sector's role as a socioeconomic agent in the city and across the region.

The Impetus Plan was comprehensive. It included a detailed process for identifying structural problems within the sector and outlined a plan of action that included everything from improving access to investment capital to improving democratic management and the ways in which social economy organizations communicate their stories to the world. Integral to this process was the transformation of Barcelona Activa, the city's enterprise development center, with programs and personnel promoting the social economy and co-operative enterprise. Barcelona Activa became the interface between the City proper and the social economy. The strategy called for closer integration and co-operation among the various elements of the social economy as well as closer collaboration among City departments. Throughout, Barcelona En Comu understood the importance of autonomy and self-direction for the social economy. The City was to play a facilitative and enabling role while organizations of the social economy took the lead in formulating policies to strengthen the productive power of the sector.

Barcelona's efforts to elevate the social economy as a social power are among the most comprehensive and ambitious of their kind. Using frontline activists as staff within the City, Barcelona showed how a municipality could be a catalyst for change by partnering with civil institutions that embody its social, political, and economic values. In so doing, the City spurred further evolution of the social economy across the region and elevated its capacity to engage in a long-term process of social change. The plan has had an effect.

There has been a 5.4 percent increase in the number of new co-operatives in the period 2016–2018, a 25.3 percent increase in the number of enterprises transacted in the social economy network (2016–2017), and a 32 percent increase in co-operatives registered in the Federation of Worker Cooperatives of Catalonia (FCTC). In this period also, a Network of Co-operative Athenaeums of Catalonia was formed, as was the Network of Social Economy Municipalities (XMESS). An inclusive platform of the entire social economy was created, the Association of Worker-Owned Enterprises and Social Economy of Catalonia (ASESCAT) was formed, and the process for passing a Law of Social and Solidarity Economy of Catalonia was put into motion.[7]

◆ ◆ ◆

Participatory democracy was a second pillar of Barcelona en Comu's political program, and the party's use of online technology marked a new frontier in democratic governance. The creation of Decidim, a digital platform for democratic decision-making, became a powerful tool in En Comu's efforts to engage the citizenry in the public affairs of the city. It was not confined to matters of municipal governance. Decidim was designed to support the democratic process for any purpose and by any organization. It is a free software system that promotes collaboration, and its licensing protocol protects it as a digital commons. Since its inception, Decidim has become its own online democratic community. Its ultimate purpose is the cultivation of democratic culture.

In 2016–2017, Decidim was used to design strategic planning for the city. In the course of this process, there were more than 80 citizen assemblies and over 8,000 citizen proposals for improving the quality of life in the city. Over 70 percent of these proposals were accepted, and Decidim is used to track, evaluate, and revise the projects.

Currently, more than 150 organizations use Decidim for managing all aspects of participation and decision-making. It is a key resource for the social economy, and over 40,000 people are registered on the platform. Climate activists are using the platform to promote their activities and to engage citizens in discussions to improve the environment. After four years, more than 2,000 meetings had been documented on the system, which includes a huge archive of citizen participation in the city. As a deliberative system, Decidim plays a key role, but, as Arnau Monterde of Decidim has said:

> Decidim is important, but the political commitment to authentic participation is even more important. What is essential is the commitment to place real political discussions and issues on the table. This relates to the commitment to implementing political values. One must never separate technology from politics. Citizen participation is not just a technological question…it is a political process. A political institution needs more than the small number of power brokers and professionals that direct decisions and implement actions. It's important to find specific ways that people with different types of knowledge can enter into the political decision-making process. The challenge is how to design a state machine that has access to civil knowledge.

Ultimately, the purpose of Decidim is to promote the democratic culture and governance of a community. In combination with Barcelona En Comu's other public engagement actions, it appears to have succeeded. Decidim has increased the level of civic participation by as much as twenty times. People feel like they have more influence over policy. It has also allowed the City to connect with people that have never before engaged in public life.

Today, Decidim has been expanded to 80 cities, 20 countries, 150 organizations, the Catalan government, social economy groups and co-ops across Spain and Europe.

◆   ◆   ◆

The premise of an individual's "right to the city" and the goal of encouraging in citizens a process of "personal flowering" through engagement in public life is a deep social process. As Amartya Sen has said, the common life of the city—what makes a city liveable—is inseparable from the fulfillment of personal freedom. Conversely, what makes personal freedom possible is the presence of those conditions that offer both the scope and the capacity for individuals to act. As we saw, this idea has its roots in the Aristotelian conception of the city as the institution through which an individual may realize their full potential—both as an individual and as a social being.

According to Sen, the freedom to pursue such a flowering is a precondition of happiness and the only value that truly measures the well-being of a community. Justice does not depend on the treatment accorded to individuals by institutions or by political power. It derives from the "ethical and cultural ties that unite the individual to society and creates an atmosphere of freedom...the overall environment in which individual choices make sense."[8] But happiness is not a personal attainment. Happiness emerges in an environment where the well-being of community and the individual are interdependent—a *social* process, not a product of atomized action based solely on self-interest as in the liberal ideal.

The modern city, managed as a collection of services to be "delivered" to citizens, is a corporate archetype grafted onto the social body of the community. When citizens are referred to as "clients" and when politicians talk about services in terms borrowed from business culture (value for money, cost efficiency, "deliverables," etc.), the city is reduced to mere bureaucracy. It's organic connection to citizens as active, conscious contributors to a living community are erased. This corporate conception of the city isolates people in passivity and impotence. Their identity as citizens belonging to a political community is stolen. It is the end product of a continuous process of desocialization, transforming the city into a space hospitable only to commercial culture and personal consumption. The effects are predictable.

Researchers at the Annette Strauss Institute for Civic Life at the University of Texas relate the decline of civil and political engagement to a corresponding decline in other key areas: absence of civility in public debate, lowered attention to public affairs, decline

of positive role models, and the decline of civic and political skills[9]—
the kinds of skills that can only be cultivated when people are engaged in civil affairs.

In any community, levels of trust and faith in public institutions
are linked to the degree in which members of a community are engaged in civic life. Decline in civic engagement results in a decline
in social capital, which in turn undermines civic life in a downward
spiral of deteriorating conditions for the community. As pointed out
in the report of the Strauss Institute's Social Capital Project, "high
levels of civic engagement are associated with better public governance. An atomized society with limited capacity for cooperation is
no society at all. It will face economic stagnation or decline relative
to others in which members work together."[10]

Like Barcelona En Comu, civil mobilizations the world over have
focused on the city as the most favourable terrain for realizing the
democratic values they espouse. In city after city, experimentation
in new forms of urban commons and the expansion of co-operative
modes of governance and citizen participation are the building
blocks of a new imaginary for reclaiming communal life in the city.
In essence, Barcelona is modelling a municipal-level analog of the
Partner State.

THE WAY OF THE PEASANT

Globalize the Struggle—Globalize Hope
— La Via Campesina slogan

WHEN NAGARIKANTI YELLAIAH walked out to his small plot one day in January 1998, it seemed a routine chore for the young Indian farmer. Instead, holding a small bottle of insecticide, he lay down in his field and drank the organophosphate poison. It worked fast on the nervous system. His pupils shrank to pinpoints, his vision blurred, and soaked in sweat and vomiting, he went into convulsions before finally expiring from respiratory arrest. Death would have come painfully. His body was found in his failed crop, which was still being attacked by worms and caterpillars. Twelve hours later, villagers found Bennala Venkateswarlu with a bottle of insecticide lying beside him. By April, 350 farmers had hanged themselves or drunk the poisons that had failed to save their crops.[1] Like Nagarikanti, most of them came from the Warangal district in Andhra Pradesh, one of India's biggest cotton-growing areas.

In 2019, 42,480 farmers in India died by suicide.[2] They are casualties of a war that has pitted the small farmers of the world against the Goliaths of corporate agriculture. The peasant farmers of India, like their brethren in countries across the globe, are paying the ultimate price of "progress" that has transformed the food systems of the world. It is the unfolding of a global catastrophe that is radically altering not only the food we eat but the ecosystems and lifeways that have sustained rural economies and peasant families for millennia.

Death and despair are one outcome of this process. Defiance and mass resistance is another.

◆ ◆ ◆

Few organizations can lay claim to representing the hopes and struggles of the majority of the world's population. La Via Campesina is one. Since its inception, Via Campesina has become the most powerful grassroots force in the anti-globalization or *altermundista* ("another world") movement. With 182 member organizations in 81 countries, it is also the world's largest. Its membership represents over 500 million peasant families and Indigenous people across five continents. The literal meaning of the name is "the way of the peasant."

A true peasant's international, and a leading force in the struggle to reverse the scourge of neoliberalism around the world, Via Campesina's experience sheds a unique light on the global role that civil power can play for change in our era.

Contrary to what one might expect from inside the high-tech, urban bubble that frames our perception of the world, it is peasant organizations and peasant sensibilities that are formulating the most incisive critiques of globalization and advancing meaningful alternatives. The fight for survival waged by Indigenous people in the rain forests of Brazil or farmers in India has given birth to a new collective identity—a peasant identity—and given shape and voice to a global vision for political action.

The emergence of Via Campesina is tied to the changing role of the nation-state in rural societies—particularly in the global South—and the decline of the state as a protector of peasant rights. Like the peasant and worker movements that were prompted by the social wreckage of industrial capitalism in the 1800s, Via Campesina is emblematic of this same struggle in our time and at global scale.

Latin America has the most unequal distribution of land and income in the world. It also experienced the steepest decline in living standards when a combination of neoliberal policies and plummeting commodity prices ravaged the region during the "lost decade" of the 1980s. A continent-wide process of peasant mobilization started to take shape in this period. A turning point was reached in 1990 in the course of region-wide protests against the celebrations planned for the quincentennial of Columbus's arrival in America. Rejecting the official narrative of "discovery" and the civilizing mission of European colonization, the Declaration of Quito was formulated to recognize "500 Years of Indian Resistance" and to establish the basis of a transnational peasant movement.[3] In this seminal document, the participants expressed a deep concern for the destruction of nature and proposed what Stefano Varese calls the "moral management of the cosmos" or "moral ecology":

> We do not own nature…it is not a commodity…it is an integral part of our life; it is our past, present, and future. We believe that this meaning of humanity and of the environment is not only valid for our communities of Indo-American people. We believe that this form of life is an option and a light for the people of the world oppressed by a system which dominates people and nature.[4]

According to Varese, the "ecological cosmology of rural communities, based on the notion and practice of individual usufruct of collective property and the primacy of use value, resisted…the intrusion of a cosmology based on exchange value that corresponded to the capitalist market economy."[5] In essence, peasant lifeways preserve the collective forms of rural economies from a previous era while adapting to meet the contemporary demands of global capitalism.

We recognize Varese's notion of moral economy. It embodies the values of collective ownership, of common rights and obligations, of use value over commodity value, and of the primacy of co-operation, reciprocity, and the common good. In this moral economy, economic relations are based on the logic of reciprocity and production for sustenance. It acknowledges interdependence between the individual and their community and between humanity and the natural world. These same principles are also embedded in the idea of *Buen Vivir* that was also formulated in the South—a holistic view of political economy that may be translated as "Good Living"—that describes a way of life that is community-centric, ecologically balanced, and culturally sensitive. In this view, nature has rights with legal protections—it cannot be treated as mere property.

An economy founded on moral principles is what the international peasant movement is struggling to bring into the global debate about the future of agriculture and, more broadly, as a counter-vision to free-market capitalism. Karl Polanyi and the theoreticians of cooperative economics would have felt at home here. What is new in this formulation is the explicit links that the peasant movement has made to the issues of environment and sustainability.

The Quito Declaration, and the admixture of peoples and process that brought it forth, signalled a turning point for popular struggle in Latin America. A new collective identity of the oppressed was being forged. To this point, peasant movements in Latin America were deeply bound to the structures of domination from which they were struggling to break free. The public services provided to rural populations after WWII were often used by governments to create clientelist relations that kept many peasant organizations and their leadership hostage to state patronage and the political parties that controlled state funding.

As in Latin America, peasant organizations in Africa and Asia became extensions of particular political parties who could deliver the patronage spoils of political power. Agricultural subsidies, crop quotas, monopolies on markets and distribution channels, these policy goods were all dispensed as political favours in return for rural votes. Political parties across the ideological spectrum—from communist, to socialist, to Christian Democrat—were able to cultivate their corresponding peasant organizations. Peasant leaders were defined by their ability to negotiate client relationships with power brokers in the urban centers. Peasant organizations subordinated the interests of their members in structural change to the urban interests of political parties in maintaining the status quo.

All this changed with the advent of monoculture and the domination of export markets. With the rise of global agro-industry and the entry of high-tech into agricultural production, the WTO, the World Bank, and the IMF changed the rules of the game. The social control of capital through state regulation was dismantled. "Structural adjustment" policies marginalized the role of the state, and as political parties and their client peasant organizations became even more irrelevant, a new breed of peasant organization came to the fore.

Lessons had been learned. The new groupings were more militant, the leadership less compromised, and the organizations more independent from the influence of political parties, government offices, the church, and NGOs whose outlook and allegiances were often at odds with the activist aims of the peasants.[6] Peasant groups demanded a restoration of the state services slashed by neoliberal policies. They fought for agrarian reform and for the creation of national markets that could restore peasant agriculture and resist the monopolies that had taken control of food systems. It became apparent that the focus of the movement had to extend beyond the national state. National problems in agriculture, as in so many other areas, cannot be solved at purely national levels if the forces that produce these problems operate globally. A new systemic, internationalist approach was needed. It also required the forging of a collective identity rooted in the peasant experience.

The making of this collective, and now transnational, consciousness was indelibly shaped by the centuries-long struggle for survival and self-worth that was a permanent feature of the slow extermination process that unfolded over centuries of colonial conquest.

In his work, *The Making of the English Working Class*, E. P. Thompson describes a very similar process in the formation of a collective class identity for the working class of England in the formative years 1780–1832. In the preface, he claims "in the years between 1780 and 1832 most English working people came to feel an identity of interests as between themselves, and as against other men whose interests are different from (and usually opposed to) their's." Thompson's avowed aim was to "rescue the poor stockinger, the Luddite cropper, the 'obsolete' hand-loom weaver, the 'utopian' artisan…from the enormous condescension of posterity." The global struggle of the peasant movement today, and the making of its own collective identity, is also to rescue itself—and perhaps us—from the nihilism and condescension of the present.

At a global gathering in Managua in 1992, peasant groups from Central America, the Caribbean, North America, and Europe met to deliberate on the impacts of neoliberalism on agriculture and their communities. They articulated a "common frame of meaning" that rejected the brutal consequences of industrial agriculture—free trade, low prices, dispossession, and the growing impoverishment of the countryside. They concluded that an alternative model was desperately needed, and that food and agricultural policies that affected their communities must be articulated and led by peasants themselves. It was at this gathering of the National Union of Farmers and Cattle Ranchers, or UNAG, that Via Campesina was born.

Via Campesina has given peasants a global voice and a global presence. It is a poor people's movement, a movement of the marginalized and the threatened. It has embraced this identity and turned it into a weapon of affirmation and resistance. The movement has staked out its terrain. It will allow only authentic, grassroots-based peasant organizations into its membership. It does not accept resources that compromise its freedom of action or permit any interference in internal decisions. Independence, autonomy, and accountability to its membership base are sacrosanct. It is a political stance and operating outlook that has been forged through hard lessons.

The movement is confrontational, demanding, uncompromising, and not very polite. It muscles its way into rooms and around tables where decisions affecting their members are being made. It is well-informed and knows what it is talking about. It is blunt, unapologetic about its worldview, and advances clear, consistent proposals. It is very effective. Its great strengths are clarity of vision, global reach twinned with local accountability, and, above all, the ability to put thousands of its members into the streets, which it does frequently and seemingly tirelessly. It is a global pain in the ass.

◆ ◆ ◆

The concept of food sovereignty is perhaps the best means of illustrating the role Via Campesina has played as a force for system change. Food sovereignty entered the political lexicon at the World Food Summit in 1996 when Via Campesina advanced the concept as an alternative way of framing our understanding of food systems. Food sovereignty refutes the notion that peasant life and traditional forms of small-scale agriculture are the remnants of a bygone, precapitalist era. Today, the term has gained worldwide currency throughout civil society and across political and economic institutions.

Food sovereignty has its ideological roots not in the colonial cultures of the North but in the experiences and political struggles of the peasant movements. Its approach is one of social transformation and reflects a life experience rooted to the soil and the sustenance of the natural world. Its ideology is grounded on the social ethics of equality, reciprocity, and the common good.

Far from considering traditional rural values and lifeways as obsolete, Via Campesina relates the precapitalist past with a possible— indeed necessary—postcapitalist future. It is not advocating for a nostalgic return to a premodern age; it is proposing an alternative path for modernity.

Food sovereignty means the right of peoples to healthy and culturally appropriate food produced through ecologically sound and sustainable methods, and the right of communities, as well as governments, to define and control their food systems. These policies are a frontal attack on the monopoly power of transnational corporations and on the trade policies that sustain these monopolies.

The fight to assert food sovereignty is also a struggle to assert a new conception of *human rights*. The traditional conception of human rights is rooted in the liberal, Enlightenment tradition of the

West in which rights are essentially individualistic and expressed in the individual's freedom to act as an economic and political subject. Food sovereignty proposes a conception of *collective* rights, in which collective identity and collective control over the means of food production reframe rights as cultural and societal imperatives. Collective rights are those individual rights that belong to the individual as a member of a community. It is the community *as a whole* that embodies these rights and exercises them through the agency of each individual member. In turn, the notion of collective rights is inseparable from the idea of the commons and of the common good. The battle to apply food sovereignty to international trade rules and to protect collective rights against the power of transnational corporations is where the real war is now being waged.

The fight for food sovereignty is the front line against the corporate takeover of the world food system. Without food sovereignty, it is a question of time before the final dispossession of the remaining independent farmers of the world is complete. This means the commodification and destruction of all remaining wilderness lands and, like the privatization of the world's water, corporate control over the essential sources of human life.

Via Campesina's focus on food sovereignty has enormous significance for peasant mobilization. It signals the transition from a disparate collection of peasant revolts to a coherent and unified peasant movement. This entails a unifying vision and the organizational capacity to mobilize at unprecedented levels. Second, it signals the emergence of an autonomous peasant self-identity and the intellectual power to give this identity form and voice. Third, food sovereignty is a transformative symbol. It establishes the means by which popular mobilization translates into political power through the enactment of ideas that necessitate substantive societal transformation.

In its methods, Via Campesina shares the values of horizontality, autonomy, and direct democracy that characterize other mass mobilizations of our era. But its conception of system change, articulated in the language of rights and based on the matrix of food, provides a coherence and clarity of vision that has been missing from many of the mass movements to date. Via Campesina has shown that mass mobilization can be sustained over time and at global scale. This, too, is in contrast to the ephemerality of so many of the mass mobilizations in the last twenty years. How has Via Campesina accomplished this? And what are the lessons that might be gleaned for meeting the challenge of governability in an age of globalized power?

Glocalism

Via Campesina's power ultimately rests on strong, locally based rural movements that mobilize for food sovereignty and peasant rights in their own territory. Its claim to be representative also depends on the participatory and democratic decision-making structures of these diverse organizations that work together at the regional level. Through its ability to combine regional communication and co-ordination with transnational strategies for collective action, Via Campesina uses its bottom-up structure and its inclusive ways of working to reinforce collective action. Consensus building, although often slow and cumbersome, is essential to building solidarity and a sense of collective identity and common purpose.

This linkage of the local with the global and the ability to harness mass mobilization to a vision of change through an effective political strategy are crucial lessons for making civil mobilization effective in the age of globalized power. Perhaps the best way to appreciate this is through the global campaign now being waged to protect the free and open sharing of seeds—the foundation of all food systems. Via Campesina, through its leadership, its political analysis, and its global reach has been a key force in this epic struggle.

◆ ◆ ◆

From time immemorial, farmers have freely selected, saved, and exchanged seeds. Access to seeds has been the basis of a global agricultural commons that links food production to the natural life systems that are the common inheritance of all peoples. Today, this system is being overturned by the efforts of agribusiness to patent seeds and privatize their use. Under the pretext of improving seed productivity, agribusiness is causing the loss of three quarters of seed diversity and undermining a seed pool that has taken 10,000 years of agricultural experience to produce.

Three companies, Bayer, Syngenta, and Corteva, control more than 50 percent of the world's commercial seeds, which are then genetically modified to resist the herbicides and pesticides also produced by these companies. Under the impetus of the WTO, the World Bank, and the IMF, and through free trade agreements and laws protecting seed and breeders' rights, this proprietary system only allows the circulation of its own seeds, criminalizing the saving, exchange, donation, and sale of local farmer seeds.[7] From the perspective of seed companies, the age-old practice of saving and sharing seeds represents a loss of potential income. Patented hybrid seeds are the answer. Designed to withstand the chemical fertilizers and pesticides that are now universally used in industrial farming, these hybrid seeds are the basis of a production system oriented around monoculture and hyper profits.

Genetically modified (GM) seeds cannot be replanted. They must be repurchased by the farmer every year. They are designed to make the farmer utterly dependent on corporations for access to seeds as well as the chemical products that allow them to grow. According to Greenpeace, Monsanto sells 90 percent of GM seeds worldwide, but its seed monopoly extends far beyond food. Monsanto also controls 95 percent of the cotton seed market. In places like India, this has been catastrophic for cotton farmers. For mega corporations like Monsanto, however, this is pure malign genius— a monopoly over a life source that is ensured and engineered into the very product they sell.[8]

The privatization of seeds is the endgame in the extermination of the autonomous farmer and the means by which the corporate takeover of the world food system will be completed. As Vandana Shiva has said, "Control over seed, the first link in the food chain, is control over life."[9] For the small farmers of Via Campesina, this is a life-and-death struggle. Without seed freedom, there is no independent farming—much less food sovereignty.

Monsanto entered the Indian seed sector in 1988, when the World Bank and the IMF required the Government of India to dismantle its state-owned seed supply system. The passage of the new Seed Policy was just one of the "structural adjustment" policies that was demanded in return for the £19 billion in loans granted to the government. India was also forced to end subsidies, close public agriculture institutions, and provide incentives for the growing of "cash crops" to earn foreign exchange. It was the beginning of the end for traditional farming in India.

Seed has a life-sustaining significance for India's 500 million farmers. Traditionally, almost 80 percent of Indian seed, the best of each year's crop, is collected and replanted. Wrapped in age-old ritual, every stage of its lifecycle—from germination to harvest—is prayed for and celebrated. Saving, sharing, and reusing seed are fundamental freedoms and the source of rural life itself.

The Green Revolution of the 70s and 80s promised to solve the world's hunger by offering higher yields through industrial farming and biotechnology. It accelerated the transition of Indian farming from subsistence and local consumption to the growing of cash crops for export. Cotton was the golden crop. Over the last twenty years, millions of farmers have been seduced by aggressive advertising campaigns and incentives to switch to cotton with promises of quick riches obtained through the use of patented Bt seeds. Companies claim that the seeds can increase crop yields by 8 percent and generate a 30 percent gain in profit. For poor farmers, these kinds of promises are hard to resist.

India is the world's second-largest cotton producer after China. The country cultivates more than 9 million hectares, and cotton earns almost a third of the nation's foreign exchange. Cotton employs more than a million farmers. It is also the bridgehead into India's vast food system. The use of patented GM cottonseeds is the spearhead for the eventual takeover of the Indian seed supply. It is also linked to the suicides of more than 300,000 Indian farmers since the introduction of genetically modified seeds in the 1990s.

◆　◆　◆

The Warangal district in central India where Nagarikanti took his life is a dry semi-feudal land cultivated for centuries by subsistence farmers. Some of the land was tilled for cotton, some for a variety of other crops that helped feed the families and to grow produce for sale in local markets. Seduced by corporate advertising and encouraged with state incentives, farmers here began switching to cotton as a monoculture crop to cash in on the increased yields promised by the seeds they were now required to purchase. The fertilizer merchants, the pesticide dealers, and the moneylenders soon followed. Often, the same Monsanto sales agent filled these roles.

But the seeds they bought were unreliable. They were expensive, and farmers had to pay royalties for using them and often went into debt to pay for them. They also needed more water than traditional seeds, and the pesticides that the seeds needed to grow bred chemical-resistant superbugs. Farmers had to pay royalties for using them. The price of cotton could fall. In the winter of 1998, in one of the worst outbreaks of pests and disease in years, all these disasters struck at once. Countless small farmers were wiped out.

Activist Vandana Shiva has dubbed Monsanto's patented seeds "suicide seeds." According to Vasuki Berlavadi, who works for a group representing 50,000 farmers, "The seeds can be bad. And the pesticides are often diluted by the people who sell them. Cotton is get-rich-quick farming, like gambling. Once people are in debt, they must go on growing it. If they don't pay their debts, they will commit suicide, too. It happens in a weak moment."[10] Meanwhile, the price of seed has vaulted 8,000 percent.

Debt is the single-largest cause of suicides among farmers in India. And, while debt has always been a depressing fact of village life in India, the transition to GM seeds has caused farmer debt to skyrocket. In the past, farmer debt was largely in the hands of local moneylenders. The beneficiaries today are mega corporations that profit from the inputs needed to sustain the farming methods they control and the royalties they gather from the seeds they sell. The damage they have done is incalculable. According to the Food and Agriculture Organization, during the course of the 20th century,

75 percent of crop diversity has been lost. Before the introduction of biotechnology in India, there were roughly 50,000 rice varieties. Within twenty years, this number has dropped to a mere 40. In India, 15 million cultivators have abandoned their fields since 1995.[11]

There is no question that this story paints a very gloomy picture. Opposition to the forces that are pushing such a pestilential model into the world is a question of survival for the millions of small farmers that still produce 70 percent of the world's food supply. Agriculture is still the number one source of employment and livelihood for half the world's population. But to plumb the depths of the depravity that is being unleashed into the world, we must follow the trajectory of the biochemical agribusiness model to its logical conclusion. We find this is in the development of Genetic Use Restriction Technology (GURT), or what have been more vividly described as terminator seeds.

Terminator seeds are genetically designed to produce plants that are sterile. This would ensure that farmers could not reuse them and thus guarantee the "protection" of intellectual property rights that supposedly inhere in the seeds. The seeds were originally developed in the 1990s through the collaboration of the U.S. Department of Agriculture (USDA) and Delta & Pine Land, a company that was later purchased by Monsanto. Here's how Willard Phelps, an official spokesman for the USDA described the scheme:

> Our system is a way of self-policing the unauthorized use of American technology. It's similar to copyright protection.... This technology is designed to increase the value of proprietary seed owned by US seed companies and to open up new markets in Second and Third World countries.[12]

"The new technology will be so widely developed that future farmers will be able to purchase only sterile seed."[13]

The government's rationale was that companies would otherwise cease to invest in future technologies if they could not be assured of a return on their investment. But it wasn't only companies that stood to gain from the technology. The USDA scientists working on the project would also personally receive a portion of the profits. The USDA planned to make the terminator technology available to all seed companies as early as 2004.

Terminator seeds produce sterile plants and then die off. There are now new patents on Genetically Driven Organisms (GDOs) that not only produce sterility in the source organism but also spread to produce sterility in other target organisms. When news of this technology got out, the public response was swift and uncompromising. La Via Campesina provided a crucial organizational vehicle to mobilize civil action at scale.

Facing universal condemnation and protests around the world, the UN was forced to impose a global moratorium under the UN's Convention on Biological Diversity (CBD) in 2000. The mobilizations continued.

On April 17 2002,[14] Via Campesina and a wide field of NGOs, human rights groups, and environmentalists took to the streets in huge numbers. They filled auditoriums, briefed politicians, engaged in land occupations, and organized teach-ins. In the Netherlands, Via Campesina leaders from Indonesia and Bangladesh joined Dutch farmers and activists to take over a genetically modified seed test site and converted it to a sustainable biodiversity site. Following news of the contamination of corn in Mexico by genetically modified plants, farmers and activists throughout the Americas launched a weeklong continental campaign against GMOs. In Guatemala and Brazil where the struggle over seeds is linked to land reform, Indigenous peasant organizations occupied fifteen estates in Guatemala and demonstrated for continuous land occupations across nine states in Brazil.[15]

The alliance of Via Campesina peasant organizations with other civil organizations that joined the food sovereignty campaign was crucial in stemming the introduction of terminator technology. But the victory, while significant, was vulnerable. The UN convention was aggressively challenged in 2005 and 2006 by, among others, Canada and New Zealand. It can hold so long as concerted civil action such as that fronted by Via Campesina and its allies can maintain a global focus, concentrate pressure on strategic targets, develop alternative policies, and continue to mobilize action with precision at all levels—from the local county to the UN council chamber. And, while moratoria are crucial to stemming destructive practices, the United Nations needs a monitoring and evaluation mechanism that would allow it to track new technologies as they move from discovery to diffusion and before commercialization.

The role of organizations like Via Campesina that have the capacity to follow events at multiple levels and mobilize action when necessary is crucial in this respect. Direct participation in the monitoring and review process by those directly affected by such technologies is imperative. In turn, this requires the presence of civil organizations that are capable of playing such a role. Broad public awareness and education are central to these efforts as they enable the conjoining of local action to issues of global reach. Just as important are a vision of what constitutes an alternative path forward and a means of embedding policy and practice into an ideology of change. Food sovereignty is one such ideology.

And lest we are lulled into believing that the destruction of farming is just the hard fate that falls to some poor villager in a backward country, it is exactly the same process that is causing the disappearance of independent farms and the death of rural communities in the prosperous North. Across huge swathes of the U.S., Canada, and Europe, what were once vibrant rural communities are now ghost towns surrounded by vast tracts of corporate farms, growing unthinkable amounts of GM crops, saturated with insecticides and chemical fertilizers and worked on by a handful of company employees—all that is required by the automated systems and robotic machines that now tend the empty fields.

As in the global South, the dehumanization of agriculture in the North demands a humanizing response for the future. In its vision and its organization, Via Campesina reflects what a new modernity might mean. Local sovereignty, democratic values, global awareness linked to local practice, and the embrace of ecology posit a modernity that links livelihoods to a reverence for nature and the revisioning of humanity as an extension, not a master, of the natural world.

6

DEEP DEMOCRACY IN KERALA

I N AD 52, THE APOSTLE THOMAS set sail from Judea to spread the gospel message to India. His route took him to Alexandria where he boarded a riverboat and, following the spice route, sailed down the Nile as far as Koptos and thence by caravan over the desert sands to Berenike on the shores of the Red Sea. He then sailed down the Red Sea and, skirting the tip of what is today Yemen, slipped out to the wide breast of the Indian Ocean to arrive finally at the spice trading centre of Cranganore on the Malabar coast of Kerala. From here, ships of the Roman merchant fleet would bring pepper, cinnamon, and slave girls to the markets of the Mediterranean and the Black Sea.

Thomas's message found fertile spiritual soil. The Christian communities he founded are among the world's oldest. Thomas founded eight churches before being murdered in Madras by a Brahmin priest. He could not have known how his mission would affect not only the spiritual lives of his converts but even more profoundly the material conditions of life for millions that followed. Two millennia later, the Syrian Christians became the catalysts of a social upheaval that changed the face of Kerala.[1]

❖ ❖ ❖

Much has been made of Kerala's placement inside India's chaotic political firmament. With the country's highest standards in health, literacy, women's rights, infant survival, equality, and life expectancy, Kerala is at the top of India's quality of life index. These achievements have been made despite a relatively low level of economic development. Indeed, Kerala's development model is the opposite of what neoliberalism prescribes. It isn't industrialization and economic growth that produced the high quality of life. It is state leadership, an empowered civil society, and collective action aimed squarely at social and economic transformation. At a time when global warming demands alternatives to growth, the example of Kerala has global significance.

The key to Kerala's success was the state's focus on governance. Kerala's accomplishments are closely linked to decentralization and the expansion of democratic practice. Deep democracy, as it was pursued in Kerala, had two critical implications. One was a critique of conventional Marxist practice and its glorification of the state as the *repository* of reform, and the second was a rebuttal of the anarchist view of the state as an invalid *agent* of reform.

The dynamic role of a strong civil society and a government's capacity to institutionalize democratic renewal are the key lessons of this story.

The Channar Revolt

The Parayans dwell at the bottom of the caste system in Kerala. They are among India's Untouchables—literally *outcasts*, subhumans who were associated with the "unclean" occupations that were performed by its members. These included the lowest forms of manual labor and association with bodies, meat, blood, cleaning, pest control, etc. The caste system in India is a finely calibrated index of status, and the lower down the caste ladder one descends, the darker the skin colour. Caste discrimination and exploitation in India reads like a graduated color chart. There are today some 100 million Untouchables, or Dalits, living in India—an underclass like no other.

Parayans were not only untouchable, they were also *unseeable*—they could not allow themselves to be seen or be in proximity to higher castes. The English word "pariah" comes from *Parayan*—for good reason. The prohibitions against contact or even proximity to Parayans were calculated with precision. Violation of this taboo was punishable by death.

Parayans could not touch anything that the higher castes touched. If a Parayan's shadow fell on a Brahmin, the Brahmin must bathe to wash away the impurity. Parayans were expected to crawl backwards with a broom, sweeping away their footprints so that Brahmins would not accidently be defiled by stepping into a Parayan's footprints. Like other Untouchables, Parayans were not allowed on public roads or to carry umbrellas, or to enter temples. They could not cover their dwellings with a roof. They could not be literate or enter a school or obtain an education. They could not use public wells. They, like other Hindus, could not marry outside their caste. When they spoke, they had to cover their mouths so that they would not pollute those whom they addressed. And Parayan women, like other women of low caste, were prohibited from covering their breasts.

Exposed breasts were a humiliating mark of subservience. Incredible as it will seem, all lower caste women were subject to a breast tax, the *Mulakaram*. An official would go from door to door collecting a tax on any woman past the age of puberty who wanted to cover her breasts. Tax collectors levied the tax according to the size of a woman's breasts. The official would determine the tax by handling the woman's breasts with his hands. It was perhaps the most disgusting tax ever imposed on women.

The Syrian Christians also adhered to the rules of untouchability; however, unlike Hindus, Syrian Christian women were allowed to cover their breasts—a judicious application of the Christian doctrine of equality before God (at least among men) and no doubt prompted by the scandalized sensibilities of the English missionaries. The right to cover one's breasts was the spark that lit the fire of reform in South India.

It was a revolt by the Nadar women that marked a turning point in the fight for equal rights. The Nadar are a large subcaste whose traditional occupation was tree climbing. The Nadar climbers would

scale the palm trees of Kerala to harvest the coconuts and palm
leaves that were essential to the rural economy and way of life. Using
a series of caterpillar like motions, climbers would inch their way
up trunks rising thirty metres or more. It is a meagre and precarious
living where falls are common, as are fatalities and life-destroying
disabilities.

Many Nadar women had converted to Christianity, often to escape the scourge of untouchability. Seeing their Christian sisters
wearing the long-sleeved jacket that covered their upper bodies,
Nadar women began wearing the long top cloth, the *channar* that
was worn by upper caste Hindus. The backlash was as vicious as
it was predictable. In the markets, upper caste Hindu men tore
the cloth from the women's bodies. More delicately minded men,
respecting the caste proscriptions against proximity, attached ma-
chetes to long poles and sliced the clothing from the women's bodies
while standing at a safe distance. In one case, when two covered
Nadar women were walking to market, an official had them stripped
and hung from a tree in public view.[2]

The women's response was equally swift and uncompromising.
They looted shops and unleashed a fury of pent-up rage that terror-
ized upper caste neighborhoods and villages. The revolt caught and
spread. Soon, low caste Hindu women also joined in the protest and
started wearing the body cloth worn by upper caste women. The revolt spread from Kerala to neighbouring Tamil Nadu and across the
south. The dam of caste privilege was cracking, and the floodwaters
of reform were seeping through.

On July 26, 1859, following a half-century of struggle, the Maha-
raja of Travancore issued a decree granting the right of Nadar women
to cover their breasts. It was the first major victory for women's rights
in India. This landmark victory is now seen as the seminal event that
gave impetus to the social movements that shaped modern Kerala.
The wave of reform set in motion by the Nadar women changed the
face of Kerala from that of a feudal Brahmin backwater to one of the
most progressive polities in the developing world. Youth, students,

women, peasants, trade unions, political parties, reformers, spiritual leaders, and public intellectuals were all caught up in the ferment.

What transpired in Kerala during this formative period was a monumental experiment in the cultural, social, and political transformation of a society—without recourse to the force of arms. But it was the broader array of reform movements that had sprung into being, independently of the political parties, that ultimately propelled the long struggle for reform—regardless of who held power in government.

Modernity in Kerala was a product not of capitalist development as envisioned in the Western model of industrialization, nor on the centralized planning role of the state as decreed in the conventional socialist archetype. It was a product of radical democratizing pressures from below and the formation of state policies that responded positively to these pressures. In the process, ideas concerning the state, the role of government, and the act of governing were profoundly changed.

❖ ❖ ❖

In 1957, the Communist Party of India was carried to power as Kerala's first elected administration following independence. It was the first elected socialist government in the West, and the reforms that it introduced were radical and far-reaching. They included land reform, wealth redistribution, health and social care reform, and the promotion of universal public education and literacy. However, the reform process reached far beyond individual policies or programs. It included a determined effort to deepen democracy within the decision-making structures of the state itself.

The move to decentralize political power and to mobilize mass participation in government reflects how the administration viewed the relation between social reform and the state. It was in stark contrast to the traditional approach whereby the apparatus of the state was placed in the hands of the Party, which then directed decisions from the center. Democratization in Kerala attempted the opposite.

It linked civil society into the decision-making processes of the state. The role of the state was to facilitate this process. Decentralization and direct decision-making by citizens were applied widely—from the reform of health and social care to boosting economic development. Moreover, owing to the strength and organization of civil power, this process has survived regardless of the party that has held power in government.

It was in the area of planning that decentralization found its classic expression as an instrument of mass mobilization and as an experiment in state/civil society partnership. From the outset, civil society organizations played a decisive role in the conceptualization of Kerala's democratization project and its organization. The People's Campaign for Decentralized Planning was launched in 1996, conceived as a vehicle both to deepen democracy and to spur economic development. This required not only radical changes in how the institutions of government *operated* but also changes in how people *behaved*. Institutional change depended on the evolution of people's values, orienting them toward democracy and hence to the transformation of their social relations.[3]

The end goals were the deepening of deliberative democracy and a new synergy between state and civil society. Considering the social divisions and inequalities described above, it was a monumental vision. Special attention was devoted to the most marginalized in society—women, the lowest castes, and the scheduled tribes.

The People's Campaign began with the mobilization of people into citizens' assemblies, or *gram sabhas*, at the level of the village council, or *panchayat*. Success here depended on addressing two issues that were crucial to engaging the populace: raising awareness and proper preparation. To this end, a massive training program was launched, accompanied by intensive media campaigns, popular theatre performances, and conferences. Over a thousand resource persons were mobilized and trained to act as facilitators in the discussion groups.

The first citizen assembly was organized on September 15, 1996, with great fanfare in the coastal town of Trivandrum, the capital of

Kerala. Adorned with British colonial architecture and set against a green blue sea and blazing white beaches, the town came alive with countless residents, government officials, politicians, activists, party organizers, and villagers gathering in their thousands in the first of a long series of social dialogues that were unprecedented in India. Over the following months, village and ward assemblies were the main events all over Kerala. In village after village, set among the emerald seas of rice paddies and coconut palms, it is estimated that more than two million people took part in these assemblies. The gatherings sparked public debate on planning across the whole of Kerala and became the primary focus of political and social life in the state. The role of civil society organizations, which provided volunteers and organizing expertise, was essential to the success of the mobilization.

From the vantage point of public awareness and mobilizing a populace, the assemblies were an astounding success, with participation strongest in the rural areas. Still, the turnout for women, lower caste members, and members of the scheduled tribes was disappointingly low. Despite this, the generation of a statewide debate on issues that touched the daily lives and concerns of a populace at this level was a stupendous achievement. As described by Rashmi Sharma, it was "a far cry from both the vote-gathering rhetoric and protest-against-government around which public mobilization usually takes place. In terms of its educative value alone, the exercise is remarkable."[4]

But there was a great deal yet to learn. Initial assumptions about planning, popular mobilization, principles of participation, and the role of training and technical expertise had to be revised. It was soon found that decentralization sometimes undermined effective planning. Some decisions were not conducive to being made at a local level. The local pressures that compel village councils to address people's basic needs do not necessarily work for longer-term projects or larger-scale planning.

Some problems are simply beyond the capacity of local government bodies and civil organizations to address. In these cases,

decentralization amounts to an abrogation of responsibility for deal-
ing with complex issues such as reducing unemployment, addressing
pollution, or promoting industry—all of which are profoundly felt at
the local level but with little of the institutional capacity or technical
expertise needed to address these questions locally. There was an
urgent need to match technical expertise to the kinds of projects that
were being identified. Basic skills such as budgeting and financial
management were often lacking.

Moreover, the devolution of funds to local control entails a vastly
more complex system of administration, information sharing, and
oversight than simpler centralized systems. Fully 50 percent of state
funds had been devolved to the local levels for disbursement. Decentralization often served to complicate planning decisions and to frag-
ment available human and financial resources, sometimes producing
contradictory or redundant effects.

Also, the grim realities of existing social relations and power
alignments bubbled to the surface. Local politicians demanded a
set-aside of funds that they could disburse independently of the
planning priorities set by the assemblies. Officials of the centralized
bureaucracy were reluctant to hand over decision-making power to
citizens. The perennial problem of institutional self-interest and inertia reared its head.

Despite these handicaps, the process persevered and changes
were made. Things improved. Skilled help was harnessed to the
planning work of local bodies and task forces. The development
work was executed faster and with more confidence. At the same
time, there was significant improvement in the milk and vegetable
production of the state. The improvement of village council infrastructure was one consequence of the People's Campaign. The availability of equipment and resources such as computers, buildings, fax
machines, telephones, and vehicles was greater for Kerala government organizations and departments than that of any other state
in India.

The People's Campaign was a herculean undertaking, and its effects were deep and long-lasting. Among its greatest achievements

was the decentralization of health care and the creation of Primary Health Centres to serve rural areas. Health care was extended to everyone regardless of income level, caste, tribe, or gender. Communities were brought together to determine which health issues were a priority and needed attention, with topics ranging from strengthening local health facilities to improving water and sanitation safety.[5] While the national government was promoting the privatization of health care, Kerala expanded the public health service and established trust between the health services and the populace. All this was to prove crucial to Kerala's handling of the pandemic.

The development priorities of the first communist administration reflected a worldview and political strategy that had taken shape over decades. The communist party had mobilized the subaltern classes around a reformist agenda that challenged both the caste divides of traditional society and the exploitative conditions that remained as stubborn holdovers from a feudal past. Decentralization and the deepening of democratic practice and political culture were woven into the mobilizations of the People's Campaign. But these ideas were equally present in the bitter battles to enact education and land reform and the wider struggle to promote economic, gender, and social justice.

In the case of land reform, what was accomplished in Kerala far exceeded similar efforts in the rest of India. Close to two million acres were redistributed from landlords to 1.3 million households. The impact of the reforms on landlessness was enormous. In 1959, one-third of the rural households owned no land; by the 1980s, 92.2 percent of rural labor households owned land. As Oommen noted, Kerala "had the unique distinction among Indian states of having abolished feudal landlordism, lock, stock, and barrel."[6]

Access to land allowed a historically abject class that included artisans, farm servants, and agricultural laborers to gain title to their hutment land, to gain some security of food and income, and to decrease their state of utter dependency. Untouchables also demanded the right to sit like human beings when receiving instructions from their landlords, instead of squatting in the dirt like animals.[7]

The mass mobilizations around planning on land and education reform brought a silent and subjugated underclass into the political process and into the collective life of a deeply stratified society. Its members internalized the rights to which they were entitled and gave voice to them. And while the democratizing process was implemented by the state, it needed the help of activist organizations in civil society to bring it to fruition.

The achievements of Kerala are acknowledged and admired. But the results, while obvious in such areas as health, literacy, education, and basic infrastructure, were weaker in the area of economic development. What perplexed many was the apparent contradiction between a high level of social well-being, far surpassing the levels of other countries in the global South, and a relatively low level of economic development. This contradicts development orthodoxy, which claims that high levels of social development are a consequence of high levels of economic development—particularly *industrial* development. The Kerala experience proved this false.

It is not necessary to wait for economic growth to improve the material conditions of life. It is inequality and the exploitative social relations in a society that determine the limits to individual and social well-being. The redistribution of land or access to basic health and education are political choices—not economic outcomes. Kerala's example forces us to rethink the relation between economic development and social welfare—particularly in the context of global warming. Planning for sustainability and the prospect of de-growth and shrinking economies requires us to seek out models that achieve basic standards of social well-being and quality of life without high levels of growth—precisely what Kerala has achieved.

Kudumbashree

In the lush green landscape of Kerala's backcountry, a line of brightly clad women walks in single file along a path separating a turned field of rich red earth on one side from a banana grove on the other. The broad emerald-coloured leaves of the banana plants catch the afternoon light and, bending to the breeze, blaze bright against the deeper green of the forest wall at the far edge of the field. At their head, a tiny figure works her way up a rise, bracing her heavy hands against her knees for leverage. Her feet are hard and worn and cracked like old leather. With her iron-grey hair pulled back from a round friendly face, Jaanki is a shy, smiling 60-year-old matron who worked as a farm laborer in Chengannur, in the interior of the state. It is a region known for its red earth, its black pepper, and an ancient Syrian Christian church that was built over 1,650 years ago.

For the past seven years, Jaanki has been part of a small band of women who pooled their money and purchased this small patch of earth to grow bananas and cultivate the plot jointly as a co-operative. The farm is one of the 70,000 *sangha krishis*—collective farms—that have sprouted with the assistance of Kudumbashree, a vast network of productive enterprises that is the product of India's largest and most ambitious effort to eradicate poverty among women. With help from Kudumbashree, the farming collectives grow paddy, tapioca, tuber crops, ginger, vegetables, and spices, turning barren land into fertile and productive fields. Over 10 million acres have been brought into cultivation through collective farming.[8]

Despite a chronic shortage of locally produced food, this land had lain fallow. Food had to be imported from outside the state. Kudumbashree saw the unused land as an opportunity to employ women and to generate livelihoods. The organization pressured the state to lease the land to farm groups. With plots averaging less than 2.5 acres, there are now over a quarter of a million women farmers in Kerala cultivating land in common. Echoing the practices of La Via Campesina, these women run their farms on the principle of "food justice"—surplus produce can be sold on the market only after all the families of the group farm have satisfied their own needs.

The success of these co-operative small farms far exceeds anything else in India. In one district, the repayment rate on loans taken by co-op members to run their farms is 98.5 percent.[9] Kudumbashree's relationship with the Kerala Development Bank, in combination with local credit circles, means that these women and their families can work their farms and avoid the grip of local moneylenders. In many villages, Kudumbashree is the largest depositor in the local bank.[10]

Countless enterprises, both collective and privately owned, have been supported by the organization. The businesses are registered as Kudumbashree members and are linked to a nested system of supports that provides them with the skills and resources they need to succeed. Farm groups receive subsidies, seeds, natural fertilizer, micro-loans, and the training necessary to work their collective farms using organic methods.

Kudumbashree was conceived as a joint program between the state of Kerala and civil society organizations. It operates via a network of community-based organizations (CBOs) of poor women, with the CBOs functioning as a wing of local government. The CBO system has a three-tier structure. At the primary level, neighbourhood groups (NHGs) are organized with 10 to 20 members composed of women drawn primarily from poor families. These NHGs are then affiliated to an area development society (ADS) at the ward level. All the ADSs in a Panchayat/Municipality are then federated under a community development society (CDS), which is registered with the local self government (LSG). Fully 60 percent of the women in Kerala belong to Kudumbashree. With 4.5 million members, it is an astonishing achievement of state-initiated civil organization and mobilization and likely the largest gender justice and poverty reduction program in the world.

The neighbourhood groups meet weekly in the houses of members. At these meetings, all the members bring their savings that are then pooled and redistributed as loans to group members. Each group has its own designated officers, which are responsible for the day-to-day management of the group's affairs. Each neighbourhood group then elects a representative to sit on the area development society at the ward level. The general body of the ADS consists of all presidents, secretaries, and three sectoral volunteers of the federated NHGs. In addition, the system provides for proportional representation from the lowest castes and scheduled tribes as well as designated vulnerable groups.

The Kudumbashree system is regulated by a bylaw that establishes not only the working mechanism of the system but, crucially, the ways in which civil society interacts with the state around mutually defined goals. Kudumbashree is therefore far more than a delivery mechanism for an anti-poverty program. It is a designated space and structure for ensuring a constant dialogue between the distinctive roles and powers of government on the one hand and broader civil society on the other. In key ways, this structured interface between civil society and the governance apparatus of the state embodies essential features of what we will examine later as the Partner State. Kerala is a prime example of how a model of co-operative civil/state governance functions in real life.

For the vast majority of women, Kudumbashree was the first entry into a public life. Many had never ventured beyond the stifling precincts of the household. Most had never belonged to a social group. Their new status as independent earners granted them a new standing within the household and in the community. As one respondent noted in a study, "Earlier I used to consult my husband for each and every thing before taking a decision...but now that I have my own money, I take most of the decisions regarding household." This is small, tangible, life-changing power.

Kudumbashree is not free of problems. This newfound empowerment has also resulted in cases of women that won't let go of their power as elected reps once they have tasted it. Elected positions are often transformed into permanent postings. Kudumbashree has to guard against encroaching bureaucratization and corruption. Many NHGs do not honour the two-year electoral term. When the program scaled up from a pilot to statewide application, CBOs began to see it as a government operation and felt entitled to remuneration. Kudumbashree's ability to mobilize millions of women made it a coveted political prize. Political parties and religious groups with their own agendas try to infiltrate the organization with people interested more in promoting ideologies than fighting poverty.[11] The organization has a huge following, deep roots, and wide recognition and respect. It carries political clout.

Many of these issues are also present in the decentralization process itself. Many observers have noted the influence of political partisanship and bias in how planning decisions are made, and for whose benefit. Bureaucratic intransigence and power hoarding are alive and well. But in a culture where caste hierarchy and clientelism are the twin rails of social standing and the pathway to success, it is little wonder that democratization would be resisted by politicians and civil officials at all levels.

Such resistance is in the DNA of hierarchical structures. Those who manage these systems owe their positions and the benefits they enjoy precisely to the hoarding of power. The Indian bureaucracy is the preferred habitat of the petty tyrant—whether in Kerala or anywhere else. In a caste system like India's, government bureaucracy reflects and reinforces social hierarchy. Despite all this, what is remarkable in Kerala is the extent to which decentralization and the deepening of democracy through the empowerment of civil society have succeeded.

The decentralization project, along with the economic empowerment of women, has gone a long way to transforming one of India's most caste-ridden and inequitable societies. The campaigns to equalize access to education, to improve literacy, to redistribute land, and to improve health have all contributed to this process. Today, caste discrimination, once among the worst in India, is lower in Kerala than almost anywhere else. Religious bigotry and intolerance, while spreading like a plague in other parts of the country, is relatively rare. The politics of division and disinformation that fuelled Prime Minister Modi's landslide victory in the federal election of 2019 had little purchase in Kerala. Modi did not win a single seat in the state. When he arrived in Trivandrum after the elections to pump up his followers and to claim Kerala as his own, he was met with protests and told to go home.

It is impossible to say with certainty to what degree the democratizing efforts of the state contributed to the emergence of these cultural and social traits in Kerala. We can only compare the evidence of the recent past with the realities of the present and the differences manifested in the lived experience of Keralites and how this measures against the realities now unfolding across the rest of India. It is a sight that gives one both hope and despair. On the one hand, the drumbeat of a resurgent Hindu nationalism is drowning out the voice of tolerance, which has always been a feature of India's religious and cultural heritage. But Kerala's continuing commitment to social equality indicates that the century-long struggle for social reform has established a bridgehead against bigotry and ignorance. And, while the continuing erosion of civil rights at the national level corresponds to the centralization of authoritarian control in the hands of Modi and his circle, the decentralization of political power and decision-making in Kerala has institutionalized civil power and established grassroots political engagement as an assumed right of citizenship.

Economic empowerment—whether in the form of redistributed land ownership or in the training and gainful employment of women—transforms people's social relations and political outlook. In the case of Kerala, an enlightened state has chosen continuous democratization as the pathway to social and economic advancement. And while its progress in economic development has not matched its social achievements, Kerala's populace enjoys a standard of life unmatched in the rest of India and among the highest in the developing world.

This is not owing to the munificence of the state. It is a synergy between the institutions of state and the revolutionary aims of a mobilized civil society. These mobilizations preceded the rise of a formal political movement represented by the political parties. This is a central lesson of the Kerala experience. Civil society established a social benchmark that governments of both the left and the right have to meet if they wish to govern. In Kerala, social justice is the fruit of a creative tension between organized civil power within the broader society and its representation—however imperfectly— within the governance structures of the state.

The institutionalization of civil power outside the power structures of the state is hardly perfect, but it is deep and durable. One of the most consequential lessons for us from Kerala is that social justice and collective well-being are not the by-products of an expanding capitalist economy as neoliberalism would like us to believe. It is the product of a sustained popular struggle to equalize social and economic relations and to institutionalize civil power by democratizing the governance and decision-making apparatus of the state. We can have a decent society if, instead of fetishizing a growth where wealth is siphoned off by elites, we invest in the social transformations that minimize the replication of elites altogether.

LIVING WITHOUT APPROVAL:
STATELESS DEMOCRACY IN ROJAVA[1]

In our narrative so far, the fundamental role of the nation-state has been taken for granted. Whether it is the mass movements calling for social, economic, and political change or the efforts in Spain or Kerala to democratize the political system, the state has been either the object or the agent of these reformist efforts. The assumption has been that the state is *reformable*—that it is capable of embodying, or at least advancing, the political values that underpin these efforts.

Perhaps this is a delusion.

The revolution that is taking place in northeast Syria believes it is. Democratic confederalism in Rojava views the state *itself* as the problem. Capitalism and the nation-state, far from being in opposition, are two aspects of a single overarching system of violence and inequality that defines the modern era. Democratic confederalism proposes an alternative model of modernity based on the greatest possible extension of democracy—a *stateless* democracy that systematically disassembles the structures of centralized state power.

What is happening in northeast Syria is possibly the world's most ambitious attempt to establish a co-operative form of political economy based on direct democracy, gender equality, and ecology. It has done so by abandoning the notion of a nation-state. It is the only real democracy in the Middle East, and it is fighting for its life.

◆ ◆ ◆

Rojava captured the world's attention in the fall of 2014 when the Kurdish city of Kobane came under siege from ISIS.[2] Up to this point, the advance of ISIS in Syria had seemed unstoppable, spreading terror and trailing horror across the region. The world had watched as a string of beheadings and other atrocities flooded airwaves and social media—part of a calculated campaign to sow terror by appalling the imagination. Could anything be worse than Al-Qaeda or the Taliban? Yes, it turns out. In the terror sweepstakes, ISIS was setting a new standard for depravity.

From October 2014 to March 2015, Kurdish forces slowly repelled the ISIS attack on Kobane with the support of U.S. air strikes and reinforcements from Kurdish fighters in Turkey and Iraq and the Syrian Democratic Forces (SDF). In savage door-to-door fighting, defenders on the ground would relay co-ordinates to U.S. bombers who would then target ISIS militants dug into the city. With the destruction of one building, Kurdish forces would advance and occupy the site and then send co-ordinates for the next run, slowly retaking the terrain.

The repulsion of ISIS at Kobane handed the jihadists their first defeat. In the wake of their retreat, ISIS left a trail of massacred civilians, raped women, and heaps of headless bodies.[3] But the myth of ISIS's invincibility was shattered. Equally significant, the defeat had come at the hands of women. The YPJ, the Women's Protection Units, had fought alongside the men of the YPG, People's Protection Units, the heart of the Kurdish militia. For the misogynist ISIS, it was a double humiliation. And with the fame won by the women combatants of the YPJ, the world saw for the first time the feminist face of the struggle. With victory, one senses the glee of YPJ commander Ruken Jirik, when she had this to say:

> Jihadists have little fear of death because they think they are going straight to heaven. They carry a key to paradise around their necks and a spoon on the belts to eat with Mohammed. But they are terrified of being killed by a woman because

then they will not go to paradise. They fear women fighters. Fighters of the YPJ will trill to let them know who they are fighting against.[4]

That fear, it turns out, was well-founded. The bone-chilling ululations rising from the YPJ pursued ISIS until its final defeat in Raqqa in October 2017.

It has now been ten blood-soaked years since the eruption of the Syrian conflict. What began as a peaceful movement for political and economic reform has given way to a proxy war of competing interests invested in sectarian control of the region. In November 2012, ISIS forces entered Syria from Turkey at the border town of Serekaniye, with the full knowledge and blessings of the Turkish state. Turkey has used ISIS and other jihadist forces as cat's paws in its power plays in Syria ever since. In March 2018, Turkish forces invaded Afrin and, with the aid of Islamist armed gangs, commenced an immediate campaign of ethnic cleansing, kidnappings, rape, and repression. It is estimated that half of Syria's population has been displaced by the conflict. Many of those fleeing sought refuge in Rojava, the Kurdish region of northeast Syria.

The Kurds of Rojava

Syria is a patchwork nation. Perhaps the most ethnically diverse of the Middle East states, its people are composed of Sunni and Shi'a Muslims, Ismailis, Alawi, Druze, Greek Orthodox, Turkmen, Maronite and other Christian sects. Among the oldest inhabitants of this region are the Kurds. Their traditional homeland, Kurdistan, stretches across the northern rim of Syria and extends into Turkey to the north and Iraq and Iran on the east. The creation of Syria, like that of the other Middle East states, was a product of the European powers' division of the former Ottoman lands following defeat of the empire in WWI. Kurdistan was carved up and divided among four newly minted nations. The result in Syria was that the region's Kurds found themselves cut off from their ancestral lands in Turkey and Iraq. The borders drawn by the French authorities imposed on the Kurdish population new social and political identities that were ethnically, linguistically, and culturally alien.

In Turkey and Syria, Kurds were denied recognition as a distinct people. Their language was banned, their music was silenced, and a policy of sustained cultural extermination was imposed that continues to this day. With a population of 40 million, the Kurds are the world's largest stateless ethnic group. The Kurds have never given up on regaining a homeland.

Rojava means "Western Kurdistan." It is comprised of the three cantons of Afrin, Kobane, and Jazira in northeast Syria. In January 2014, the three cantons declared their autonomy and succeeded in establishing a revolutionary administrative authority that now controls the predominantly Kurdish region in the north of Syria as well as non-Kurdish territory to the south. Given the history of the Kurdish struggle for recognition and the innumerable possible catastrophes that might have come from the collapse of the Syrian regime in this area, it is a remarkable outcome. This is not only because of the emergence of a particular Kurdish political identity in this war-torn region but even more because of its character.

◆ ◆ ◆

The political vision that has guided the revolutionary movement in northeast Syria is Democratic Confederalism, a political philosophy expounded by Abdullah Öcalan, the founder of the Kurdistan Workers' Party in Turkey (PKK) and guiding inspiration for the revolution. When he founded the PKK in 1978, Öcalan was a traditional Marxist. He was aiming for a centralist, socialist state for the Kurds and fought for its establishment throughout the 1980s. But after the collapse of socialism in the Soviet Union in 1991, the PKK faced a crisis in its aims and political outlook. The party underwent a profound re-orientation of its socialist values and embraced a version of democratic socialism that broke with orthodox Marxist-Leninist political theory. Öcalan, in particular, confronted this dilemma through a re-evaluation of his own thinking and sought a new way forward. A deconstruction of the state and top-down power structures was at the heart of this process. The Kurdish Women's Movement played a pivotal role in this effort. Öcalan was deeply influenced by feminist political thinking, and gender equality became a foundational principle in his philosophy.

The core of this change was the radical reappraisal and rejection of the state. It is the central thesis of the Democratic Union Party (PYD) in Syria, a sister party to the PKK in Turkey and the most powerful political force in Rojava. The adoption of a feminist political critique, stateless direct democracy, and a focus on ecology made the PKK in Turkey among the most innovative and forward-looking leftist organizations in the world. Until it emerged as a political project of the PYD in Rojava, Democratic Confederalism remained largely unknown to the outside world.

Democratic Confederalism

Democratic Confederalism[5] describes the political theory of stateless democracy in northeast Syria. It was first adopted by the PYD in 2007, and when the Syrian government forces withdrew from Rojava in March 2011, the model was applied across the whole of the Kurdish territory.

Democratic Conferederalism advocates universal and direct democracy as the foundation of a free society and rejects the state as a precondition for its realization. This understanding of democratic self-government is *inclusive*—granting democratic rights to all peoples living in a region regardless of ethnicity or religion; *egalitarian*—particularly as it applies to gender equality and the emancipation of women as full citizens; *autonomous*—recognizing the right of communities to govern themselves; and *ecological*—recognizing the co-dependence of human societies with nature and the need to protect her. These principles establish the framework for the governance system of the Autonomous Administration of North and East Syria and are embedded in the Social Contract, the constitution of the region.

In Democratic Confederalism, the idea of the "nation" is based solely on the practice of democratic citizenship. It is divorced from the standard conception of the nation as a collectivity based on ethnicity or language or, indeed, any other form of collective identity. In the context of a Kurdish identity that is itself segmented and understood variously by different groups at different times, this is of immense significance. All societies are inherently heterogeneous. This diversity of interests, identities, inclinations, and worldviews can be subsumed into a unitary collective identity only through an act of communal mythmaking and coercion. From the perspective of Democratic Confederalism, this process violates the natural composition of human societies and the freedom of individuals.

Öcalan put it this way:

> Democratic Federalism is the offspring of the life of the society. The state continuously orients itself towards centralism in order to pursue the interests of the power monopolies. Just the opposite is true for confederalism. Not the monopolies but the society is at the center of political focus. The heterogeneous structure of the society is in contradiction to all forms of centralism. Distinct centralism only results in social eruptions. Within living memory people have always formed loose groups of clans, tribes, or other communities with federal qualities. In this way they were able to preserve their internal autonomy.... The centralist model is not an administrative model wanted by the society. Instead, it has its source in the preservation of the power of monopolies.[6]

We are accustomed to thinking of democracy as a form of government operating through the institutions of the state. But what does a stateless democracy even look like?

In the cases of Barcelona En Comu in Spain and the communist administrations of Kerala, democratization, decentralization, and citizen participation defined how these efforts sought to reform politics. The same is true of La Via Campesina and its distributed form of decision-making. The mobilization of civil power is central to all these efforts. In the cases of Spain and Kerala, ultimate authority still resides in the hands of the state and is exercised through the elected officials of a representative government. Regardless of the degree of citizen engagement, legitimate power is always vested in the institutions of the state: in its executive, judicial, and legislative functions and in the enforcement mechanism of its various armed forces, from police to military. The bureaucratic apparatus is also firmly under the control of the ministers and appointees of the state. Civil society remains an outside force: perhaps consulted, perhaps mobilized into collective action, perhaps engaging with various levels of government on matters of policy and decision-making. But formal power always flows outward from the center and down from an established hierarchy within the state.

Democratic confederalism reverses this process. In Öcalan's vision, ultimate control is vested in the institutions of civil society by delegating to local self-governments the administrative functions as determined by society itself. Its aim is to place society in control of governance. How is this accomplished?

The Council System

The governance system of the Autonomous Administration in Rojava is a work in progress and continues to evolve as experience and circumstances dictate. The basis of this governance architecture is the council system. Self-governance and direct democracy are enacted through a series of nested decision-making bodies, which—in theory—are accountable to the levels below them and closest to the actual residents of the neighborhoods in the region's cities, towns, and villages. The Administration functions through five interlocking levels: commune, neighborhood, district, canton, and region. All of these are connected to the umbrella of the Syrian Democratic Council.[7]

The foundation of the system is the commune, which is a deliberative body encompassing 30 to 200 families in a residential street. In larger cities, a commune may have as many as 500 households. There are communes in every neighborhood and a neighborhood may have 10 to 30 communes, each composed of 15 to 50 people. Participation in these bodies is voluntary and open to all. The commune is the place where the day-to-day affairs of the residents are discussed,

where goods and services are supplied, and where solutions are ham-
mered out for common problems. According to one activist:

> The commune is the smallest unit and the basis of Demo-
> cratic Autonomy. It is concerned with meeting the needs of
> the people. Let's say you need something for your street. In
> the old system, you'd have to file a petition, which would be
> forwarded to Damascus. It could take years till someone fi-
> nally took notice and addressed it. Our system is far more
> effective. If there's a women-specific problem in the street, a
> conflict in the family, the commune tries to solve it. If the
> problem exceeds the capability of the commune to solve, it
> goes to the next level up, to the neighborhood council and
> so on.[8]

Each commune also has commissions, or committees, that attend to
specific areas of responsibility. There are nine: Women, Self-defense,
Economy, Families of Martyrs, Justice & Reconciliation, Education,
Arts & Culture, Health, and Youth & Sports. Most of the work of
the Autonomous Administration is done through these commissions, which are constituted at every level of the system.

The co-ordinating board of each commune is selected by the residents and consists of two co-chairs (one man and one woman), and
usually one man and one woman represent each of the commissions.
This gender parity is applied to every decision-making position, including the ministries of the Autonomous Administration. The co-
ordinating board convenes weekly, and its meetings are open to the
public. The members elected to the board can be recalled at any time
if they do not meet the wishes of the majority.

The next level up is the neighborhood council, which usually
comprises seven to thirty communes. The co-ordinating boards of
the local communes make up the deliberative body of the neighborhood council. At the neighborhood council, members elect the
co-ordinating board and the male co-chair. The female co-chair
is selected by the Women's Council, which also operates at every

level of the system. The neighborhood council also establishes its own commissions that operate in the same nine areas of responsibility.

The third level up is the district, which encompasses a city and the surrounding villages. The boards of the neighborhood and village councils make up the deliberative body of the district and represent their respective councils. Here again, the co-ordinating board is elected by the members, and the area commissions are formed. The co-ordinating board of the district, representing many neighborhood councils and communes, is called TEV–DEM, the Movement for a Democratic Society. It consists of 20 to 30 people and plays a central role in the political and social life of the region.

The fourth tier of the governance system is the People's Assembly, which operates at the canton level and is made up from the representation of all the district councils. As with the rest of the system, the co-ordinators of the lower level, in this case the district level, compose the deliberative body of TEV-DEM for the canton. Each TEV-DEM member, as well as other activists and specialists, become members of the nine commissions that co-ordinate activities for all of Rojava. TEV-DEM bodies operate in each of Rojava's cantons, which function autonomously.

Finally, the overarching umbrella for the entire system is the Syrian Democratic Council (SDC), which provides a political framework for the resolution of the Syrian conflict. This was the governance structure that had evolved prior to the invasion of Afrin by Turkish forces in 2018.

Following the invasion, the Syrian Democratic Council decided to form a unified administration by establishing seven autonomous civil administrations under the umbrella of the SDC.[9] At present, the Autonomous Administration of North and East Syria consists of a 70-member General Council representing the civil administrations, an Executive Council composed of the co-chairs of the seven civil administrations, and a 16-member Council of Justice to administer the justice system.

Berivan Khaled, co-chair of the Executive Council explained it this way:

> There was a need for an overarching Autonomous Adminis-
> tration of North and East Syria, to bring together these seven
> regional Administrations at the level of collective decisions,
> of common laws, to build equality in society, equality on an
> economic level, develop common perspectives, to coordinate,
> and to be a force of mediation if problems appear between
> two regions.[10]

The priorities of the SDC now are to resist the incursion of Turkish and Islamist paramilitary forces in the region and to play a meaningful role in the political process to resolve the Syrian conflict and to draft a new constitution for the country.

A New Pathway

Democratic confederalism breaks with the vision of equality as interpreted by socialist regimes as well as the liberal conception of individualized freedom. It offers an alternative philosophy—a democratic modernity—that institutionalizes the Enlightenment values of equality and liberty by mobilizing the creative energies of society through democratic practice.

For Öcalan, the practice of this philosophy is transformative. It changes the individual that takes part in its application. Democratic confederalism creates a new social identity, a "new Kurdish man" that transcends the particularities of ethnicity. Revolution entails a process of personal transformation that is inseparable from the political aims of social change. The council system puts this idea into daily practice.

This council architecture did not appear from nowhere. Its roots may be found in the council system of the tribal elders that adjudicated the affairs of traditional Kurdish society from ancient times until well into the 1960s and 70s. Throughout Kurdish history, communal values such as collectivism and mutual aid, anchored in tribal identity and autonomy, have provided a cultural bulwark against the imposition of centralized control in all its forms. Democratic confederalism, with its focus on decentralized local autonomy, is a continuation of this tradition. Its formulation as a project of social revolution took shape with the application of this model by the PKK in Turkey. When Öcalan founded the PKK in 1978, the party's goal was not merely to establish a socialist Kurdish state, but also the liberation of women and of all people in society regardless of ethnicity or political outlook. It was a universalist project of social liberation, but still based on the idea of the nation-state.

The PYD sought to de-ethnicize politics and establish a political system that was free from the centralized structures of the state and from any association of ethnicity with the idea of a nation. Traditional parties, such as the Kurdish Democratic Party of Syria, view ethnicity as a defining feature of a new political system that represents Kurdish interests in a distinctly Kurdish territory—a Syrian Kurdistan. The PYD's strategy ignores the established frontiers of state and territory altogether. Its aim is to establish Democratic confederalism wherever communities wish to adopt its principles, irrespective of ethnic or other distinctions.

The leadership in Rojava sees this system as the best means of securing a lasting peace—not only for the Kurds but also for other ethnic groups suffering under despotic rule in Syria and throughout the Middle East. The Kurds of Rojava still consider themselves as part of Syria. They reject the label of separatists, despite what others may claim.

Transforming Politics

Changing the nature and operating logic of social institutions changes the attitudes—*and aptitudes*—of the people who use them. One learns democratic practice by practicing democracy. The same is true of co-operation. In the context of a changing tribal society, this is crucial. One way of appreciating the significance of what is at work in the practice of Democratic confederalism is to use the language of social capital.

The tension between the fierce allegiances of the tribe and the difficulties that these tribal identities create between groups is the difference between bonding social capital and bridging social capital. Social capital is that store of mutual trust that enables a group or a society to work co-operatively to achieve common aims. *Bonding* social capital is what binds and defines the co-operative relationships among members of a group or community that shares a high degree of similarity. A tribe, a religious group, or an ethnic community are classic examples. *Bridging* social capital is what enables co-operation and connectivity between *a diversity* of groups.

What Democratic confederalism tries to do through the council system is to generate bridging social capital that can unite the constituent groups of the region into a new form of sovereignty— a social sovereignty. It does so by changing the character of the institutions through which the society operates. The transformation of politics is achieved through the democratic transformation of the society's economic and social relations. For Democratic confederalism, the state reproduces hierarchy, inequality, and an unfree society.

Stateless democracy promotes social freedom and the common good through the widest possible distribution of democratic practice. If local autonomy and direct democracy are the keys to transforming political and civil life, they are equally important in reimagining the ultimate aims of an economy. The co-operative economy that is taking shape in Rojava, despite its innumerable obstacles, is the economic face of democratic transformation.

This is the vision. To what extent has it been realized on the ground?

◆ ◆ ◆

Travel in the Kurdish-controlled areas of Rojava, although severely restricted by the continuous closure of the border crossings, is still the safest in Syria. The terrain here is flat, dry; a dusty yellow hue colours the landscape. Oil derricks poise like giant insects, immobile, meditative, rusting sentinels of the desert. Rojava sits atop Syria's richest oil fields. With the war and an economic embargo imposed by Turkey, Iraq, and Iran, replacement parts and supplies are impossible to get, and without access to markets, the administration has had to rebuild the economy from the ground up. Oil refineries have been repurposed to produce the diesel that runs the generators that produce the electricity. Electricity is rationed, and at night the towns and villages go dark.

From the management of energy supply to the production of food, co-operatives have taken a crucial place within Rojava's economy. Beyond being a survival strategy, co-operatives extend the principles of Democratic confederalism to the economy. While family and private enterprises are accepted as a key part of the economy, monopolies are illegal. Land that was formerly owned or expropriated by the Syrian state, or that has been recaptured from ISIS, is treated as commons and placed under the control of the communes. The land and property used by co-operatives has, in turn, been provided to co-ops by the communes who are also responsible for managing local economic affairs.

Co-operatives in Rojava are much like co-operatives everywhere. They are collectively owned and democratically controlled by their members, members each have one vote; they have an administrative body that is elected by the membership and is accountable to it; membership is open to all who accept the rules of the co-operative; and the co-operative is expected to cultivate an ethic of co-operation among its members through a variety of training and educational activities. In Rojava, specific reference is made to the equal treatment of women and the rejection of racism. In addition, there are a number of features that give co-ops in Rojava a very clear communal cast in their role as social as well as economic entities.

Co-operatives here are primarily seen as economic organizations that serve the interests of society as a whole. In the West, a co-op's purpose is usually framed as the provision of benefits to individual members. In Rojava, co-ops also serve the collective interests of the society. This is reflected in their open membership. Individuals who live in the region but are not working for the co-op may yet become members and support it. Open co-operativism is a unique feature of the system and holds important lessons for understanding the wider potential of a co-operative economy.

When I visited Rojava in March 2018, there were about a hundred co-operatives. At this writing, there is twice that number.

Kasrik Co-op

Kasrik co-op is a green oasis rising out of the baking land 120 km southwest of the city of Qamishlo. Set among furrows of brown earth, olive trees, and gardens, a group of greenhouses stands under arched canopies of plastic sheeting. Sheep browse among the tall green stalks of ripening corn. The co-op has the use of 5,000 hectares of land that was formerly owned by the state and used to grow wheat. For decades, the land was deforested to make room for monoculture, and the use of chemical fertilizers severely depleted the nutritive value of the soil.

Originally started by a group of farmers, Kasrik co-op now produces vegetables, corn, livestock, cheese, and cooking oil for the region. All produce is organic. This has required extensive re-education and training, particularly since chemical fertilizers are no longer available. Plans were underway to build additional greenhouses, to increase the co-op's flock of 1,250 sheep to 10,000, to establish local markets in the towns and villages, and to plant trees on 3,000 hectares of land provided by the commune. The administration also provided seeds, equipment, and training.

At the time I visited Kasrik, the co-op had 5,000 members and 100 workers. Their goal was to employ 1,000. The cost of a member share was 100 USD, and if they could not afford the cost, a member could work it off by contributing their labor. Anyone in the region could purchase a member share, and a limit of 10 was imposed to prevent undue concentration of control. With members from across the region purchasing shares and volunteering labor, the co-op was able to accumulate $500,000 in working capital within the first year. Workers are paid 8 percent of the value of the produce when it is sold, and the rest is reinvested in the co-op. Workers are also allocated a portion of the produce for their personal use. Like most other co-ops in Rojava, all workers are paid the same amount.

Kasrik is one of dozens of agricultural co-operatives that link producers and consumers through their common membership in the co-op. This community membership model is vital. It not only expands the pool of capital that can be mobilized for co-operatives, it builds solidarity among disparate groups. The inclusive mandate of co-operatives is a crucial tool for rebuilding a sense of community. In a highly fractured society where ethnic animosities have been cultivated for centuries, it is a highly effective strategy for building trust. And, as we will discuss shortly, it is a cornerstone strategy for healing the divisions of political polarization.

Co-operatives like Kasrik are a primary source of employment and food for the communes. Other co-ops focus on providing essential services such as energy and water. In a time of crisis, they are indispensable to the communities they serve. But their significance carries beyond the crisis of the present war to prefigure a model of political economy that could meet the demands of a truly foreboding future—not only in Syria but also for the world at large. Their focus on inclusivity, community service, equality, and ecology make the co-operatives of Rojava bedrock institutions for relating democratic autonomy to the mainsprings of economic and social life in the region. The co-operative economy being constructed in Rojava is a product of both necessity and ideology. It is a natural extension of the political philosophy of Democratic Confederalism. That it is succeeding amid the vortex of forces that conspire to defeat it is something of a miracle.

Contradictions and Conundrums

The crux of Rojava's revolutionary model is the absorption of state functions within society itself. This is ultimately what stateless democracy means. The intended purpose is to eliminate the power hierarchies and injustices that are hardwired into the institutions of the state. We must pose the question: Is this feasible? What happens when the separation of state and society is erased? In Öcalan's teaching, the governance functions normally attributed to the state are subsumed within the administrative functions of civil organizations that are directly controlled by the people of a given community. The entire apparatus of the Autonomous Administration and the council system is the embodiment of this idea.

There are two problems with this philosophy. The first is that there is no guarantee that the contradictions associated with hierarchy and the concentration of power within a state structure will not simply reappear and be diffused throughout society itself. Indeed, the problem of inequitable power could be made worse if the power structures become less visible. In the case of a state and formal government, the locus of power—its operations and abuses—are relatively clear and visible and can be identified. If these functions are absorbed within the very fabric of society, how does one resist them? How does one recognize them? Might the potency of an institutionalized but *informal* social hierarchy be even more insidious and difficult to control?

The second problem is whether Democratic confederalism can actually be put into practice absent the social attitudes and values that make its application feasible. These attitudes, as Öcalan has said, depend on the reconstruction of society and the individual through the practice of Democratic confederalism itself. Attitudinal change depends on Democratic confederalism, and the success of Democratic confederalism depends on attitudinal change. This is a paradox faced by every political movement that seeks revolutionary change but whose values are democratic. The change must be initiated and sustained by a body or a political movement that takes on this revolutionary role. That is, the role of a vanguard party or movement that, to be effective, must be a controlling power within the society. If the freedom and autonomy of society is to be an ultimate value, society itself has to have the means to maintain its autonomy and guard itself against the abuses that may arise even from this revolutionary movement, just as it must against a state. History is littered with examples of what happens when this principle is violated. One hierarchy is simply replaced by another.

If stateless democracy is the solution to statist oppression, the paradox of revolutionary change while building a sovereign civil society is the mother of political conundrums.

TEV–DEM (Tevgera Civaka Demokratik)— Movement for Democratic Society

The Movement for a Democratic Society (TEV-DEM) is an ambitious attempt to meet these challenges. TEV-DEM was created in August 2011, to organize and support the council and committee structures of direct democracy and to mobilize civil society to take on the functions envisioned in Democratic confederalism. It sought to create within civil society an organized body and a forum through which society as a whole could express itself and make its interests known—both to itself and to the structures that were set up to administer the new system of self-government.

Zelal Jeger, co-chair of TEV-DEM, described its role as follows:

> TEV-DEM organizes society outside of the Autonomous Administration. But our goal is not to be in opposition, we're not against the Autonomous Administration. Because our government is not a state, our thinking is not like that of the state. If the people have complaints, we write down the protests of society and we send them to the Autonomous Administration—we criticize it. And so, we play a complementary role to the Autonomous Administration within the system of the democratic nation. But if the Autonomous Administration doesn't listen to us, we will send a message—we will create an uprising.
>
> TEV-DEM works as an umbrella organization and an assembly for all civil society organizations such as unions and some civil associations…. Its role further extends to organizing those people who are not part of these organizations and defending the rights of the people. TEV-DEM acts as a counter-power to the Autonomous Administration, preventing it from reproducing itself as a state and protecting the values of Democratic confederalism.[11]

On the face of it, this statement describes a civil institution that mobilizes civil society politically and holds accountable the governance system to society as a whole. The ultimate aim of democratic confederalism is to make society more powerful than the institutions of governance.

In Democratic confederalism, the withering away of the state does not depend on the elimination of class, as in traditional Marxist-Leninist theory. The state is dissolved through the absorption of state functions by society through the practice of direct democracy. Direct democracy also dissolves the hierarchies of power that are perpetuated by the state. The sovereign society is autonomous and independent of any particular ideology or influence associated with any of its constituent parts. What, then, is the relation of a revolutionary movement to the society at-large and to the actual operations of political power within the body politic? The issue of where power resides and how it is controlled is central to the subject of system change, and many of its complexities are brought into focus in the case of Rojava.

Both the PYD and TEV–DEM have come in for criticism from other political parties and from actors within civil society in northeast Syria. While their accomplishments with respect to ethnic and women's rights are acknowledged, it is also claimed that TEV–DEM controls the political culture and direction of the Autonomous Administration and promotes the ideology of one particular group—the PYD and its allies beyond the borders of Syria.

Moreover, while political parties participate in the SDC, parties that do not recognize the validity of this system are not represented, nor are they acknowledged as legitimate political players. This remains a major bone of contention within the system. It has left the Autonomous Administration open to the charge of not being representative and of being controlled by the political interests of the SDF and the PYD, whose Kurdish representatives dominate the system. Charges have also been made that the administration discriminates against Arabs in some areas.[12]

Given the fact that the SDF created the system, it is not surprising that it would be a dominant force within it. Can the commitment to inclusion and the democratic sharing of power create the political space for meaningful challenges to the PYD and its allies? Time will tell, but the strife on the ground and the continuous attempts by outside interests such as Russia, Turkey, and Assad himself to undermine the system by sowing division among the tribes and ethnic groups is making the task all the more difficult.

The council system itself is also grappling with a host of structural issues. Elections have been problematic, and this has called into question the validity of the elections process. There is great disparity in how effectively councils operate, in the services they offer, and how representative they are of the local populace. As we saw in the decentralization process of Kerala, the autonomy of local councils makes the application and co-ordination of general policies difficult. The sheer complexity of the system, as anyone who has read this far might appreciate, is hard to grasp—much less operate—and the claims it makes on people's time and energy is immense. It would be unsurprising if, over time, popular participation ebbs and a small minority of people wield actual power.

These are the natural challenges of a system of autonomous direct democracy absent the centralizing institutions of a state. The question is, can they be resolved without the replication of hierarchies and power inequities within the social body itself?

Inside northeast Syria, the notions of gender equality, cultural diversity, and ecology present a challenge to traditional attitudes. The adoption of such a revolutionary value system—while generally supported—remains incomplete. Building understanding is slow, patient work, and the only way it can be sustained is through the gradual acceptance of a populace that sees in the administration a set of values and practices that provides not only ideas for a better future but actual, concrete solutions to the demands of surviving the present. Security, food, water, employment—these are bedrock issues that the administration must attend to while fighting off the deadly forces arranged against it.

Meanwhile, the work continues. Concepts like "commune" and "council" have become part of the local lexicon, and a window has opened onto another possible world. The revolution in Rojava offers more than hope and light to a long-suffering people. It opens a door to a new understanding of what deep democracy can mean and how it can be practiced. It offers a vision of modernity that, while rooted in the communal values of the past, reshapes those values for universal application by focusing on the co-operative underpinnings of community and the transformative power of self-governance.

Transcending the divisions of ethnicity and nationality, democratic confederalism bypasses our fixation on nation-states and offers a working model of radical democracy embedded in the relationships of everyday living. So long as it persists, Rojava is a beacon and an example to the oppressed and a mortal threat to oppressors.

Eventually, the bloodletting in Syria will end. What is being fought for now is for what follows. The sense of community that is being cobbled together by the PYD and its allies is premised on the belief that all peoples have the right of recognition and the freedom to live in peace. It is the one hope that democracy can offer. And it is precisely this that the despotic powers of the region are determined to snuff out.

THE WORLD UNMASKED

Our capital stock hasn't been destroyed.
Our human capital stock is ready to get back to work.
— Kevin Hassett, Trump economic advisor

It may seem like a ridiculous idea
but the only way to fight the plague is with decency.
— Dr. Rieux in Albert Camus' 1947 novel *The Plague*

WE LEARNED A GREAT DEAL when COVID-19 broke onto the world. In those opening months, it was as if the event had established for us a living geo-political laboratory that opened a window onto the great social patterns that rarely come into so sharp a focus in such a concentrated time. The pandemic was a magnifier of all the ways in which political culture and democratic values (or the absence of them) affect governance and the state's relation to the common good—the central theme of this book.

Scientists discovered early that when the coronavirus spread its havoc, its effects were total. At the microscopic level, the virus exposed and exploited the sicknesses latent in the human body. In the world at-large, the pandemic unmasked the ugly realities that lay beneath the comforting skin of appearances in daily life. COVID-19 acted like a political X-ray, exposing the disorders of our present condition, and the diagnosis for the future was not good.

The pandemic was a calling card from the biosphere, showing just how catastrophic are the effects of habitat loss. Seventy-five percent of pathogens infecting human populations are zoonotic—they jump from animals to humans. Habitat loss means that the transmission of diseases between human and wildlife populations rises. According to the UN, the incidence of pandemics will increase unless the destructiveness of human activity on the environment is reversed. This includes radical measures to curb the loss of biodiversity, to reduce global warming, to end intensive agriculture, to reduce meat consumption, and to stop the appalling effects of resource extraction—all of which are essential to an economic system that is insulated from its human and environmental consequences. The UN report also highlights the crucial role of public health and public infrastructure in responding to future threats. The pandemic has forced us to confront these issues as never before—not as individuals acting alone, nor yet as nations, but as a global community.

The initial response by governments varied widely. Some, like China, covered up what was happening only to impose lockdown later. Some went into lockdown right away, like Greece and New Zealand. Others went straight into denial, like the U.S. and Brazil. Some didn't know what the hell they were about, like the U.K.

The effectiveness of government efforts to contain the contagion has also varied. But what emerged was a dual portrait of the pandemic. One shows a pattern of initial outbreak followed by concerted government action and the eventual decline of infections. The other shows an escalation of contagion accompanied by government inaction and denial. Which of the two trends prevailed depended primarily on whether a government treated the pandemic as a public health crisis—and acted accordingly—or as a political issue for which partisan interests took precedence—not public health. The social attitude of populations—their willingness to conform individual behavior to the wider social good—is also a key factor. These two factors—the behavior of governments and the disposition of their populations—are, of course, interconnected.

Statistics comparing the courses of the pandemic in the East and the West make this clear. Despite its vastly superior resources and technical capacity, infections and death rates in the West dwarfed those of countries like South Korea, Japan, and Taiwan. The West's population—roughly the U.S., Canada, and Europe—is about one billion people. South Korea, with a population of 51 million, had 600 COVID deaths by November 2020. This is close to the Asian average. At Eastern levels, that means the West *should* have seen just 12,000 deaths. In fact, half a million died, and the count continued to grow. All that was needed was to follow the East's template for controlling the contagion—lockdown, universal testing and tracing, quarantine, and above all, to give no quarter. The aim should *not* have been to flatten the curve, *but to wipe out the contagion.*[1]

What really accounts for this difference? It is not wealth or power or resources. It is something far deeper. It is the presence of a set of values that buttress social trust, solidarity, the ability to endure and pull together in a time of crisis, and a sense that we all matter— including the frail and defenseless. It means a generosity of spirit that extends beyond the narrow capitalist confines of money and the toxic self-regard of individual self-interest.[2]

❖ ❖ ❖

The role of the state has been decisive in determining the course of the contagion. If anyone doubted the relevance of government—how it regards its responsibility or how it chooses to act (or not)—those doubts dwindle when loved ones get sick or one's job disappears.

According to the International Labour Organization, 1.5 billion workers in the informal economy—nearly half of the world's most vulnerable workers—were at risk of losing their livelihoods.[3] Four hundred and thirty-six million enterprises were at risk of collapse. The pandemic increased existing inequalities, and it is the most vulnerable that suffer. Relative poverty is projected to increase globally by 34 percent among the most vulnerable workers—most of who are women—and the poorest countries in Africa and South America will be hit the hardest. According to statistics released by the UN in mid-July 2020, the new poor in Latin America and the Caribbean had reached 45 million people, with those in extreme poverty numbering 28 million. Food insecurity stalked nearly 50 percent of the population. By the fall, these figures had only grown worse, and the ultimate toll was anyone's guess. According to OXFAM's inequality report released in January 2021, it will take a decade for the worlds' poorest to recoup their losses. By contrast, the world's top 1,000 billionaires recovered in just nine months.[4]

Income inequality is driving death rates. In the U.S., the death rate among the poor, blacks, and Latinos has been twice that of whites.[5] These people are the essential workers, laboring in meat plants and picking crops, and the most exposed. Toiling at the bottom of the work pyramid, they have no job protection, no health coverage, and are the lowest paid. In our topsy-turvy world, the pandemic showed how one's importance to the economy is often in inverse proportion to one's status. Ask yourself...if you could choose between farmworkers going on strike and CEOs suddenly disappearing in a puff of smoke, which would you choose?

Meanwhile, the wealth of the billionaire class has skyrocketed. In the first three months of the pandemic, U.S. billionaire wealth increased by 20 percent, $584 billion.[6] This is more than twice the amount the federal government paid out in relief cheques to 150 million Americans. In this same period, 6.5 trillion in household income disappeared and 45.5 million Americans filed for unemployment—the largest increase in living memory. In the month of June, fully one-third of American households were unable to make their rent or mortgage payments. At the same time, the U.S. stock market was booming, and by January, U.S. billionaires had increased their wealth by 40 percent to $1.1 trillion.[7]

It is often claimed that the pandemic has changed the world around us. In truth, the pandemic only acted as an accelerant to existing trends. The pause button that the world pushed in March of 2020 gave occasion to reflect on a collective experience that is unprecedented in our lifetimes. A profound reckoning took place. Global movements are converging around the central lesson that this pandemic has shown us: that everything is connected and interdependent. Our lives and our collective well-being are part of a single unity with the natural world. Our survival depends on our recognition of this fact—not only in the face of this threat but also on our capacity to change our institutions accordingly for survival in the long term. The individualism, the winner-take-all attitude and the alienation that underlie the capitalist paradigm have culminated in this dead end. So too have the institutions of government and state that reinforce these attitudes. Our change of course must somehow reconnect people to common values, to each other, and to the sense that everything—from our economies, to our common health, to our climate—is intimately linked and that in a globalized world our survival will be common or not at all. This entails not only a change of paradigm but also a change in perception.

◆ ◆ ◆

The underlying hypothesis of this book has been that human societies must constantly grapple with the tension between two tendencies: co-operation for common benefit and competition in pursuit of self-interest. The case I have been trying to make is that the dilution and distribution of political power through democracy is how societies protect themselves from the behavior of predatory elites. The pandemic revealed in a graphic way how the actions of governments reflect and reinforce these tendencies. Even more, it showed how the role of the state, ideology, and civil power affect public attitudes and social outcomes. There are lessons here that must be internalized *collectively* if a way forward is to be found that breaks with the habits and paradigms that have brought us to this crisis.

The relation between systems of governance and the common good becomes very clear when we consider the question of public health. In democracies, elected governments have an incentive to support programs that benefit the wider public because they depend on voter support for re-election. Public health is a prime example. This is not the case in autocracies. Despotic governments rely on the support of elites and special interests. Popular power runs counter to these interests. Autocrats use the rhetoric and electoral instruments of democracy not to advance popular power but to dismantle it. The link between public health and democracy provides evidence to back up this theory.

In general, high levels of democratic practice correlate with high levels of public health.[8] The opposite is true for countries with non-democratic regimes. World data show that countries with a high democracy rating showed a life expectancy of at least 72 years; conversely, countries with a low democracy index show a life expectancy that is less than 60 years. Similarly, a 2019 study looking at data for 170 countries over a 30-year period came to the same conclusion: democracies are better at protecting public health than autocracies. With respect to the pandemic, a *Globe and Mail* report profiling the worst-performing countries showed that all nine, from Brazil to Zimbabwe, are paragons of autocracy.

What the pandemic revealed is a corollary of this principle. When democracies become *less* democratic, they bring about the same decline in public health, and public goods in general, as do other non-democratic regimes. This is evident in two countries that have become global symbols for the decline of liberal democracy in the West: the U.K. and the U.S. They joined Russia, Brazil, and India as pariah states that were banned from travel to the EU for their neglect of elementary health measures to protect against COVID-19. Right wing ideologues and political parties were leading all of these countries.[9] It is no accident.

The trade-off between public health and the economy has become the measure of the true character of a government in the course of this pandemic. The contradictions are most evident in those countries where neoliberalism is strongest. How governments act reflects how accountable they feel to the publics they are meant to serve. In Naomi Klein's terminology, the disruption brought about by crisis is an opening for *disaster capitalism*. During a crisis, capital interests collude with governments to undermine democracy and further entrench their privileges by passing measures they could not get away with otherwise. These are the symptoms of an economic system in terminal decline.

The behaviors of the Trump and Johnson administrations at the onset of the pandemic are textbook examples of this phenomenon. In the U.K., instead of utilizing the public health system and the expertise of public health professionals, Boris Johnson's first instinct was to shore up the private sector and create a parallel—and dysfunctional—private system.[10] The National Health Service (NHS), already eroded by decades of austerity, was sidelined in favour of private contractors. The result was catastrophic. The contagion skyrocketed, and the public system was further undermined. But the government's policy furthered the aims of those who want to privatize health care.

Austerity cuts and outsourcing had left the NHS fragmented and dependent on a collection of disconnected private contractors who answer to shareholders, not citizens, and whose supply chains were organized on a just-in-time business ethos designed to win contracts and maximize profits—not public health. When the pandemic hit, the supply system collapsed. When the government finally started testing—after months of delay—instead of using existing resources at its disposal, including 130 public labs, universities, and research facilities, it set up three mega-facilities whose operations were managed by the accounting firm Deloitte under a nondisclosure contract.[11]

The mega-labs ran into trouble immediately. Privately contracted drive-through centers set up to take swabs for testing were hard to access, and the tests were unreliable. At one point, 350,000 samples could not be matched to records because the centers had not logged people's NHS IDs. The Royal College of Pathologists reviewed the system and cited a damning list of failures: "poor specimen taking, poor labelling or poor transcription of details, slow result turnaround, poor quality control, lack of the result being returned to the appropriate person, inappropriate application of the result, and lack of clinical input or oversight."[12]

Without adequate testing, local councils were powerless to determine infection rates in their areas and to fashion appropriate health measures. They were flying blind.

Using the pandemic as cover, the Tory government suspended the normal procurement rules and competitive bidding for public contracts. Unsurprisingly, many of the contracts went to firms that were connected to major Tory party donors, insiders, and government ministers. As Labor member Tan Dhesi put it, the pandemic contracts were "not even privatization through the back door…the pillaging is taking place in full view."[13]

One reason for this is straightforward corruption. The other reason is ideological. A government as devoted to the primacy of the private sector as Boris Johnson's could not bring itself to support the public systems that were ready, and willing, to play their part. The purposeful undermining of the public health system was thus a huge contributing factor to the spread of the pathogen—along with the usual fecklessness and incompetence of Johnson himself. And, it turns out, it is the efficacy of public health systems that ultimately determine how well a population will weather the pandemic. In the case of the U.K., the damage done to the NHS by private contractors has eaten away at the system, like the action of termites whose hidden effects become evident when the stress of a crisis brings down the entire structure.

In the U.S., ideological blindness and the sheer maliciousness surrounding the coronavirus response surpass rational understanding. It came to light that the failure to act was deliberate. Jared Kushner, Trump's son-in-law and the de facto head of the federal COVID strategy, made a cold-blooded calculation: since the highest incidence of cases were in Democratic states, it would be politically expedient to withhold federal support and blame the fallout on state governors. The coronavirus is entirely nonpartisan, however, and immediately spread to wreak havoc in Republican states as well. And, just as in the U.K., a blind faith in the quasi-messianic powers of the market sidelined any role for government. In one instance, Kushner explained, "Free markets will solve this…that is not the role of government."[14] A more muscular, entrepreneurial mindset was called for. It was a view shared by everyone in Trump's circle. The expertise of public servants was ignored, volunteers and cronies were recruited from business circles, and what emerged was an inexperienced and ideologically driven claque of amateurs—what some career officials dubbed "the Slim-Suit Crowd."[15]

Corruption bloomed. Normal procurement protocols were ignored, nondisclosure agreements flourished, and in one case, when a deal was struck to purchase 43,000 ventilators from a Dutch company, the U.S. Treasury was billed half a billion dollars more than it should have.[16] Cynicism, political favoritism, and a fanatical faith in markets caused the death and suffering of thousands.

The worst government failures overlapped almost seamlessly with Republican administrations and, of course, within areas of federal jurisdiction under Trump's control.[17] America's notorious private health system is the antithesis of what a public health crisis demands—*if* public health is a priority. The absence of an integrated public health system, the fragmented nature of private health plans, and the dispersal of responsibility for health to the individual states made a co-ordinated response to the crisis impossible. Add in the abandonment of responsibility and leadership from the White House and there is little wonder that the U.S. became the world's epicenter for the pandemic. With only 4 percent of the world's population and 25 percent of the world's cases, the U.S. was an unchecked hothouse of disease. Only with the election of an administration that was committed to state action was this situation eventually checked.

Since the onset of the pandemic, 27 million Americans have lost their health coverage. The cost of coronavirus testing and treatment for those without health insurance ranged from 42,000 to 74,000 USD. For those *with* insurance, the best-case scenario is a cost of between 22,000 and 39,000 USD.[18] Yet, opposition to public health insurance and the repeal of the Affordable Care Act remain articles of faith for the Republican Party.

By mid-June, the death toll in the U.S. has surpassed 600,000. Coronavirus vaccines are now available, but the hollowing out of the public health system and the absence of a national strategy crippled the ability of state governments to deliver the vaccine. At this writing, 40 million Americans are in danger of losing their homes and face food insecurity. The Biden administration succeeded in passing a $1.9 trillion relief bill and not a single Republican supported it. When the first relief bill was passed in 2020, Republicans complained that public benefits were disincentives to work. For them, it isn't the threat of contagion that was worrying workers, or that their jobs have disappeared; it's that they are too lazy to work. And so once again, the old class malice re-emerges—as if we are back in the 1800s. Like then, lurking in the background, is the reliable motivator of those who depend on a wage—work or starve. Meanwhile in the U.K., 1.5 million are going at least one day without food.[19]

The pressure from business circles to reopen economies is often framed as pitting public health against a supposed "economic recovery." Like the recovery that followed the financial crisis of 2008, what we are really talking about is the restoration and deepening of the economic inequalities that prevailed before the crisis. The price of this recovery is human lives. Those regions where the lockdown has been eased too early have witnessed spikes in contagion. But there is a deeper truth. Our economic system demands human sacrifice. This pandemic merely highlights a fact that is woven into the very fabric of capitalism. The disconnect between economic health and public health is a symptom of a far deeper malaise—a crisis of values in which capitalist culture must choose between livelihood and life itself. Is it not possible, with all the wealth that societies are capable of producing, that a sustainable livelihood and a fulsome life are one and the same? This too, is what the pandemic is asking us.

The U.S. and the U.K., two of the world's wealthiest economies and, in theory, the best equipped to handle the pandemic, instead became showcases of failure. It is not wealth or technology or expertise that determine success in this context. Rather, it is the degree to which a state feels responsible to its citizenry, by the trust that a citizenry places in its government, and by the health and resilience of democratic institutions to serve the public welfare.

A decent society is not an abstraction. It's meaning is most evident in those moments when compassion, solidarity, and a concern for the collective welfare are most urgently called for—in times of crisis. It is then we see the effects of ideology and how the effort to democratize political life and institutions translates into the common good.

For one illustration, let us revisit the case of Kerala.

The government of India has chronically underinvested in public health. It has spent a mere 1.28 percent of its GDP on health, and there are only 0.7 hospital beds per 1,000 people, and only 20 health care workers per 100,000. India was not prepared for a global pandemic. Six months into the pandemic, India ranked in the top six countries in terms of per capita coronavirus infections and mortality rates. Prime Minister Modi continuously downplayed the need for state action. After the first wave of infections passed, Modi lifted restrictions. He held huge political rallies and, to appease his Hindu base, allowed the world's largest religious gathering, the Kumbh Mela, to proceed as normal. Nine million pilgrims crowded into the city of Hardiwar to bathe in the Ganges and turn the festival into a super-spreader event. This, along with Modi's massive election rallies, triggered the catastrophic second wave that engulfed the nation.[20]

Like Trump and Bolosonaro, Modi's narcissism and his rejection of expert advice created a cataclysm that collapsed the country's health system and sent death rates soaring. By April 25, India reported more than 350,00 cases over a 24-hour period, the world's highest daily total.[21] The numbers of dead overwhelmed the crematoria and burial grounds. In Delhi, corpses were burned in empty lots and public parks. Authorities received requests to cut down the trees in city parks to provide fuel to burn the dead. At night, the sky above Delhi turned incandescent with the glow of the funeral pyres.

Under Modi's autocratic leadership, the country as a whole faltered. But when the pandemic first arrived in India, Kerala emerged as a world leader.[22] It was in Kerala that the first case of COVID-19 was detected. While Prime Minister Modi called for a partial curfew and urged Indians to clap hands and bang pots to honor health workers, Kerala's chief minister announced a relief package of $270 million to aid the citizenry, with the women's organization Kudumbashree playing a key role. The package included access to loans for families through the association, higher allocations for a rural employment guarantee scheme, two months of pension payments to the elderly, free food grains, and subsidies to restaurants to provide food at reduced rates. Utility payments for water and electricity as well as interest on debt payments were suspended.

Kerala is among India's smallest states, yet it tested the highest number of samples for the virus in the country. Route maps showing where infected persons have been were published, and people who were present at those places were asked to contact the Health Department so that they could be screened and tested. The route maps were widely disseminated through social media and through GoK Direct, the government's phone app. Local government officials and health workers did the groundwork of finding people who were infected and made sure their contacts stayed in isolation.

When it became clear that the coronavirus is airborne and persists on surfaces, the state mobilized its resources to produce hand sanitizer and masks and recruited the public to undertake a mass disinfection campaign to clean public areas and buses and set up sinks in bus stations for people to wash their hands. It enlisted the help of civil society. Kudumbashree mobilized its members to produce masks. The largest trade union federation in Kerala organized workers to disinfect public spaces. Coronavirus centers were set up in vacant buildings, and people who were quarantined were fed and treated by local self governments at state expense.

For those who suffered mental distress, the government set up call centers with 140 counsellors to offer solace and provide counsel. And, while millions of migrant workers in the rest of the country had been forced by the central government to walk hundreds of miles back home during the nation-wide lockdown, Kerala opened 4,600 relief camps across the state for almost 100,000 laborers, providing free food and medical care.[23] One year later, even as the second wave was ravaging the country and cases were the second highest in India, the fatality rate in Kerala remained the lowest in the nation—largely due to these prevention measures and a robust health system providing essential services at the community level.[24] This too, was a product of Kerala's decentralization campaign.

All these actions were the fruit of decades of investing in democratic social development, of experimenting and learning from the experience of citizen education and mobilization, of promoting decentralization, and, above all, of establishing a working relationship and a sense of mutual trust between the organs of state and the institutions of civil society. The solidarity that was in evidence as state and society reacted to the contagion was not accidental. It is a product of the historical efforts to advance social justice and to establish the collective good as the foundation of state policy. It is the measure against which the performance of the state is to be judged. A more decent society, judged by its treatment of the weak and the vulnerable, is one outcome. Another is the replenishment of the society's social capital and mutual trust.

The ability of the state to support civil co-operation and facilitate collective action for the common good is central to the health and well-being of societies. These actions establish a state's legitimacy with its citizenry. They are the hallmarks of a democratic culture and make it far more likely that the populace will both listen to, *and co-operate with*, the state to pursue the common good. Civil society and the state can work as partners in a joint effort to benefit the whole of a society, not just the privileged few. The opposite is true when governments lose legitimacy or when a political ideology has become so toxic that it breeds suspicion and antipathy to the very notion of co-operation for the common welfare.

State authority, communal values, and personal agency are a complex web of factors that intersect in matters of public health. In crisis, it is essential that trust is restored to people who have a history of being ignored and whose dignity has been violated. When fear is added to the mix, resistance is reflexive.

This kind of aggrieved resistance is the case with a large percentage of the U.S. electorate today. The anti-maskers, the conspiracy theorists, and the anti-vaxxers share a common distrust of public institutions. They claim the lion's share of media attention. In the U.S., it is not surprising that these extreme forms of resistance are couched in the language of individual rights and protected freedoms. These are the frames within which personal agency can be symbolized and politicized. They are the expressions of people who are reclaiming some sense of personal control against a system that has lost all legitimacy for them. But it is more than this. The toxic individualism in which this resistance is expressed is not merely a grievance against state "control." It is the calculated product of a deliberate decades-long campaign to undermine the legitimacy of government *and* to breed the very mistrust and polarization that these expressions of outrage show. They are one part of what the pandemic is revealing about a society in crisis.

The hard work of rebuilding trust and restoring the legitimacy of public authority will take far more than the demonization of such attitudes, as justified as this may seem. What is needed is the rebuilding of public and government institutions from the ground up. Actual empowerment is not only the remedy to the politicization of what is ultimately an issue of common welfare, but also a means of restoring the social trust that is imploding under the toxic effects of powerful partisan interests. A reversal of this process requires an unprecedented long-term campaign of civil education and political reformation.

There will always remain a reactionary and deeply anti-democratic element in society that is beyond the reach of such efforts. The political task is to minimize its appeal to the far larger mass of the disaffected that see no other means by which to vent their anger and frustration. A reformed and reoriented state, aligned with progressive civil institutions, is indispensable to this process.

The social divides on display in the media are worrying and demoralizing. They absorb our attention and undermine our hope. But this is only one aspect of what the pandemic is revealing. What is less visible, but equally significant, is the sense of community and solidarity, of co-operation and mutual aid that have also arisen to meet the pandemic—despite the destructive actions of political leaders who politicized the pandemic for partisan gain.

◆ ◆ ◆

The groundswell of mutual aid during a time of crisis should not be surprising, but given the dominance of the competitive worldview, it is. If we were guided solely by the values driving free-market thinking, people should be at each other's throats. But they are not. It is true that polarization is on the rise. But it is often a product of deliberate design. As the pandemic took hold, people also showed themselves to be overwhelmingly co-operative and kind. As Peter Kropotkin, who coined the term "mutual aid" put it: "Besides the law of mutual struggle there is in nature the law of mutual aid, which, for the success of the struggle for life, and especially for the progressive evolution of the species, is far more important than the law of mutual contest."[25]

In the U.K., thousands of mutual aid groups rose up, picking up groceries, delivering prescriptions, and installing digital equipment for the elderly. The medical and science community has mobilized to pool their efforts to make every resource available to COVID researchers to fight the pandemic co-operatively. Their website, crowd fightCOVID-19, describes their aim and mission:

> This is a service for COVID-19 researchers. They only need to state a wish or a task, which can go from a simple time-intensive task to be performed (e.g., transcribe data, manually annotate images), to answering a technical question which is beyond their expertise, or to setting up a collaboration. They only need to explain their request in a few lines. Then, another scientist makes the effort of understanding that request and making it reality."[26]

Such international co-operation allowed for the discovery of effective vaccines in record time.

Similarly, the World Health Organization (WHO), the European Commission, and France launched a global program in April 2020 to ensure that all countries would get access to testing, treatment, and vaccines. COVAX is a global effort that pools the contributions of participating countries as well as researchers, businesses, foundations, and civil society to subsidize the manufacture, purchase, and distribution of vaccines. By getting rich countries to pay early for vaccines, the program would ensure that capital would be available for vaccine development and manufacture. Rich countries like Canada signed up on a 50/50 plan; for every dose of vaccine bought for themselves, a second dose was bought for the world's poorest states. Over 190 economies are part of this monumental effort, which is essentially a co-operative insurance program operating at global scale. Two billion doses of safe vaccines will be made available by the end of 2021. Of these, 1.3 billion will be reserved for delivery to 92 of the world's poorest countries.[27] By April 2021, 102 countries had received the vaccine of which 50 were low-income countries for which COVAX was their only supply.[28]

George Monbiot has summarized examples of mutual aid that indicate the breadth of what communities and groups of civic-minded people—experts and lay people alike—are doing around the world. Focusing on the co-operative production of medical equipment at the start of the pandemic, he writes:

> In just one week, a group of doctors, technicians and other experts organized themselves to design a crowdsourced ventilator, the OxVent, which can be produced from widely available parts for under £1,000. Another design, VentilatorPAL, can be manufactured for $370, according to the community of technicians that created it. The Coronavirus Tech Handbook is an open-source library pooling technologies and new organizational models for beating the pandemic. In the US, self-organized expert groups are filling some of the catastrophic gaps in public health provision, carrying out testing and tracking projects, creating directories of vulnerable people and speed-matching medical specialists with the hospitals that need them.[29]

And the list goes on. The website COVID-19 Mutual Aid UK lists thousands of such efforts around the world, with a real-time tracker that allows people to pinpoint mutual aid efforts in their own community. In my own province of British Columbia, communities are rallying to co-ordinate vital services ranging from strengthening local food systems and distributing food baskets and medicines in remote Indigenous communities to providing rent supports and distributing hygiene and prevention supplies to sex workers and people who are drug dependent. The Coming Together Facebook group linked up some 30,000 Vancouver residents to connect, share, and show solidarity in every way they can imagine. It has turned into one of Canada's most prolific grassroots relief efforts.

These actions arise spontaneously in any community during a time of crisis. They draw on the wellspring of human empathy and co-operation that is the instinctual inheritance of our species. They are not merely values consciously selected by individuals but natural behaviors that are the biological bedrock of every human society. The extent to which co-operation is the norm depends on the extent to which the behavior is nurtured by the institutions of a society. Co-operation and mutual aid endure despite concerted efforts on the part of elite interests to instil in society the *opposite* values of competition and mutual antagonism. Governments and the operations of the state in general are pivotal in determining which values—competition or co-operation—might prevail.

The pandemic is showing quite clearly how the impact of capitalist ideology, rooted in the primacy of individual self-interest and the competitive ethic, has crippled the capacity of societies to respond to an overwhelming collective threat. Beyond this, the capitalist ethic is in itself bound up in two related and mutually reinforcing dynamics: the progressive alienation of individuals from each other and the collective alienation of the human community from the natural world. Both are the consequence of an attitude of mind—a consciousness—that is fragmented, uprooted, and ultimately aimless in its capacity to respond to the challenges confronting us. The threats to human society are not merely epidemiological, or political or economic—they are existential. The liberal promise of economic prosperity and progress is no longer tenable. The appeal to stability and security that authoritarian regimes offer is a false refuge founded on fear and rage. If we are to steer a safe passage through the tumult, something else entirely is called for. We need healing solutions that reinforce *connectivity* and *commonwealth* within the human community and *communion* with the natural world.

The rebuilding of commonwealth culture is perhaps the greatest challenge that the coronavirus has bequeathed the nations of the world. This is not merely the challenge of meeting the demands of this pandemic today but the even more daunting challenge of global warming. The relationship between state and civil society and the governance systems that need to evolve is now at the center of political discourse. The values that define these systems play a paramount role for the collective welfare and the social attitudes that they engender.

In a fundamental way, it is the inadequacy—or perhaps incompleteness—of our politics that has brought us to this precipice. The original purpose of politics as a collective undertaking toward the common welfare must be restored and expanded—perhaps as a politics of redemption in this late hour. To overcome the alienation and destructiveness of capitalist civilization, we need a politics not merely of *inclusion*, which is the mantra of progressives, but a politics of *interdependence*, in which governance acknowledges the connectivity among people and between the human community and the natural world.

9

TRANSFORMATION AND INTEGRATION

THE STATE IS NEITHER monolithic nor immutable. From its beginnings as a system of centralized planning and territorial control, to the rise of the Greek polis, to the modern nation-state, the state embodies the rivalries and power relations of the social groupings that comprise it. Democracy and the rise of civil power changed the raison d'être of the state from being a mechanism of elite control to becoming the steward of a society's collective welfare. This was the ultimate aim of the democratic project. But this process is continuous. The conflict between predatory minorities and populations is a constant in all societies. Today, the disequilibrium between collective and elite interests is greater than ever before, and it is tipping societies into a new cycle of revolutionary upheaval. Whether this upheaval will result in a transformation of the capitalist paradigm into something that extends—or even preserves—the democratic idea is far from certain.

In the preceding chapters, we saw how governments and social movements in very different settings are redefining the role of the state. In Barcelona and Kerala, the focus has been on how policies are made and how citizens participate in the democratic process. In Rojava, the entire edifice of the state has been rejected and governance has been subsumed by a sovereign civil power through the practice of self-governance, confederalism, and co-operation. These experiences reflect a radical shift both in the theory of the state and in systems of governance. Each of these cases rejects hierarchy as a model of governance and combines widespread civil engagement with mechanisms of localized direct democracy. La Via Campesina and many of the mass civil mobilizations of the last twenty years share these ideals. They are the building blocks of a new political imaginary.

The movement to reimagine democracy for a global age is not going unchallenged. An authoritarian countermovement has also found its voice and is placing its own stamp on national and international politics. It too, is a global phenomenon. Across the political spectrum, what is driving these movements is a common grievance against the irrelevance of existing state institutions to satisfy the social, economic, and—I would argue—psychological needs of populations the world over.

The current unrest is unlike previous cycles of revolutionary change. The critique of the liberal state has migrated from the political margins to the mainstream. It reflects far more than dissatisfaction with particular policies. It reveals a deeper unrest: a thirst for meaning in public life, a change in the *quality and direction* of life, and for a politics of values, not platitudes. To be sure, this disaffection has also given rise to a deep polarization in society. The struggle over values also defines two very different political sensibilities. One is reactive and conservative; it seeks to defend traditional identities clustered around ethnicity, nationhood, and even gender against perceived threats. Another is subsuming existing collective identities within a wider vision of the human community as a single interdependent unity, one that is continuous with the natural world around us. It is an emerging sensibility, it is global, and it shows in the character of mass movements the world over. These movements recognize the connectivity of the issues that confront us as a species—from global warming to global inequality. It is an awakening to human interdependence and its relevance for our common survival.

From a progressive standpoint, what kind of political vision might give expression to this dynamic? What are the means by which it can be made effective in the present—not some future utopia? What is the burden of responsibility that rests on the state? On the citizenry? Can common ground be found between the disaffected on either other side of the political divide? How does this relate to the profound need to transform the kinds of attitudes *and behaviors* that have brought us to this point?

Ultimately, questions concerning the absence of meaning in public life, or the connectivity of human experience, or the transformation of political consciousness are in their nature spiritual questions—not merely questions of material ends and means. The very notion of the common good invokes this deeper sense of human connectivity, awareness, and responsibility. It is in this sense that I am speaking of spirituality—not as a particular system of beliefs or religious practices, but as an awareness and connection to the common ground of human experience and life itself. This sense of connectivity is experienced in vastly different forms. Religious belief makes this connection possible through faith and ritual, philosophy and science through reason, and—I will argue—politics through the building of community.

The spiritual dimension of politics means understanding what unites people and fostering those bonds of human empathy that serve our collective happiness and welfare. Spirituality in politics means to seek out and serve the common good. It is the foundation of any vision that seeks to change the catastrophic trajectory of human behavior in the world today. The politics of an alienated age must be a politics of communion.

Politics is in large measure a matter of values and how values drive moral choices and commitments. These questions are embedded in the social relations of any community. How people treat each other and the quality of their relationships arise out of the deeper ground of human biology, of the social imperatives of human nature, and of community itself. Morality and the concern for others operate naturally and independently of religious faith or political ideology. Conversely, as we see with depressing regularity, neither religion nor ideology is a guarantor of morality. Recognition of this deeper spiritual stratum of politics has always been integral to political thought—including that of the Enlightenment philosophers.

A great failing of the left has been to abandon this field to the religious right and to leave it to the most reactionary elements in society to fill a profound spiritual emptiness in public and political life. Is it any wonder that politics feels so irrelevant to so many? In our analysis, the question of the common good invests politics with the transformative potential so needed in these times. The first object of transformation is the state itself.

The failures that we examined in the previous chapter highlight the centrality of the state as the steward of public welfare and the inability of the neoliberal regimes to fulfil this role. The crisis of legitimacy that is confronting the state today is a failure of purpose and a betrayal of trust. It is also a turning point in the Enlightenment ideal of the state as a universal commonwealth based on natural rights and the rule of reason.

For Enlightenment philosophers like Locke and Spinoza, reason was the great unifying force that would lead to a just society. The flowering of reason in civil life was not only an expression of natural right, it was the manifestation in human affairs of an immanent universal power, or spirit. For Hegel, the state was the means by which a Universal Spirit, working through the refracted consciousness of individual persons, comes to know itself. Every individual, perceiving and acting through their own partial consciousness, participates—knowingly or not—in the great labor of a universal intelligence both to create the world and to know itself through this creation. For Hegel, the state is the culmination of this evolutionary process in human affairs. This idea of immanence in human affairs is also expressed in the notion of the Holy Spirit, which in Christianity animates the love and empathy that binds people to each other and forms the basis of our collective life in community.

But the Empire of Reason that the Enlightenment philosophers dreamed of has faltered. The Enlightenment promise of human progress has instead led to a fragmented and isolated human consciousness—an anxious and unmoored individualism that has alien-ated people from each other and from the natural world. Looking at the world today, one would be hard pressed to deny that unreason rules and that the light of reason grows dimmer by the day. And if it was once assumed that reason might light the way to universal truths, in our post-modern world, the idea of truth itself is under siege. We have entered a twilight age of alternative facts where rumor and conspiracy compete with science and the testimony of our senses. The decline of politics reflects the rise of a new barbarism. One looks in vain to see any sign of a benevolent Universal Spirit in the politics of our time.

The social breakdown we are witnessing in the U.S. and other liberal democracies is inseparable from the collapse of common frames of reference and the sense that one's personal experience draws from the same world of objective data as the experience of others. This is by design. The manipulation of information and the intent to confuse and isolate the individual are hardwired into the media we use to communicate and to make sense of the world. The echo chamber effect in which our preconceived notions are fed back to us through social media fuels the polarization that is tearing so-cieties apart. Even more insidious is the misinformation propagated by right wing media to shape in people a version of reality that sows mistrust and undermines faith in public institutions, including de-mocracy and the role of government.

Unlike at any previous time in history, people living in the same society, or even the same street, inhabit different universes. This was made evident by the 2020 elections in the U.S. Fully half of the na-tion's population inhabits a different reality than the opposing half, even as the underlying grievances that animate popular disaffection with the status quo are essentially the same. That this accumulated rage was purposely stoked to divide the populace and direct anger not at the true sources of the injustices that people feel but rather at the institutions of democracy—the press, the electoral process, gov-ernment itself—is typical of authoritarian regimes. A united popu-lace is an existential threat to autocrats and elites alike.

If our sense of a common world collapses, and if our ability to perceive what is true and common to us all is a delusion, if everything is a matter of personal interpretation and private advantage, what then is the basis for politics? What is the basis for political accountability, or for that matter, any idea of social progress or the common welfare? Discourse, the basis of community, comes to an end. This is the true meaning of Trumpism, as with all tyrannies— that truth is irrelevant. All politics is reduced to a nihilistic contest of brute force, personal advantage, and the unleashed ego. Deception, the tool of psychopaths, infects everything. It is the dark, dystopian vision of Hobbes—a war of each against all—made terrifyingly real.

If one thing is clear from the multiple crises that are converging upon us, it is that if our species is to survive, human society must somehow return to a sense of common belonging, to recover a sense of common purpose that reconnects people with each other and with the dying world around us. Reliance on human reason is not enough. We require a politics of reconstruction—a politics of relationship and commonality. The politics we are in desperate need of is one whose purpose is the creation of human connectivity and solidarity. This is the ultimate task of civil society and of the state in our time.

Throughout our narrative, we have tried to show how politics— and particularly democracy—has been the means by which people have striven to create societies that serve the common good. How this common good is defined is neither handed down from a divine source nor bestowed on a passive populace by any particular power or group within society. In a democracy, the common good is defined by people themselves, acting in common, working through those relationships of co-operation and mutuality that are the foundation of healthy communities and a functioning civil society. The case studies we have discussed show how varied and complex this process can be. But in its essence, it is always about discovering what unites people in their collective welfare and how people can be empowered to achieve it.

The attempt in Rojava to create a new kind of political sensibility—a new political subject that transcends the divide between state and civil society—is a visionary effort in this direction. So is the effort to bridge the divides that separate social groups from each other and detract from the task of rebuilding a wounded society. The commitment to political equality and a sustainable ecology is unique in this sense. It is based on a blending of two political principles: a return to the Aristotelian notion of politics as a means for realizing the common good and a recognition that political freedom relies not on what the state does but on what autonomous communities of freely co-operating individuals do for themselves. It aims not only for what Aristotle termed a political revolution—a change of those who govern—but a fundamental change of regime, a *social* revolution.

Conflict and competition define the politics of political revolution—the conquest of political power. This kind of politics freezes society inside the patterns of existing power relations and conflicting group interests. It perpetuates social division. What I wish to argue is that co-operation and mutuality define the politics of *social* revolution—a fundamental altering of a society's values and collective purpose. If competition and conflict reflect the pursuit of individual self-interest as a society's ultimate good, co-operation and human empathy express the deeper bonds of community that underlie individual well-being and the common good alike. And, whereas political revolution is a necessary condition for the pursuit of particular policies, it won't alter the underlying values that determine how societies organize and express the ultimate aims of collective life. For this, a kind of social mutation needs to happen, much as the acceptance of individual liberty and democracy by populations defined the shift from the hierarchical feudal order of the past to the age of liberalism in the 18th century.

Co-operation and Social Transformation

In his book *The Evolution of Co-operation*, Robert Axelrod uses game theory to explore the dynamics of co-operation.[1] From his study of biological systems in nature and social systems in human communities, Axelrod has shown that co-operation based on the simple principle of reciprocity can take hold and eventually form a "new normal" that can replace a culture of non-co-operation. For this to work, a number of factors have to be present.

For co-operation to take hold, one person alone is not enough. In a non-co-operative environment, what is necessary is a group of co-operators practicing reciprocity among themselves, even as they interact with non-co-operators. What is key is that these individuals discriminate between those who co-operate and those who do not. Second, for co-operation to be stable, the likelihood must be high that individuals will encounter each other in the future and that their previous actions are known. This transparency is crucial if one is to model one's behavior appropriately toward others and if non-co-operative behavior is to be discouraged. Reciprocity requires that the behavior of others is mirrored in one's own. Co-operation rests on being rewarded in kind when co-operation is offered and being sanctioned with non-co-operation when it is not.

Remarkably, these principles hold true regardless of the character of individuals or of the social setting. Individuals do not need to be rational. The evolutionary process of co-operation allows successful co-operative behaviors to thrive even if individuals do not know why or how. What is important is to know how others have behaved in the past and the ability to recognize them. This is a key reason why the size of a political community is so important. Co-operation is reinforced by the accountability that is made possible through knowledge of people's reputations and the likelihood of encounters in face-to-face communities. Axelrod also found that altruism is not needed for co-operation nor is prior trust between individuals. The use of reciprocity is enough to make non-co-operative behavior unappealing. Finally, no central authority is required to enforce co-operation—reciprocity is enough for co-operation to be self-policing.

These principles were also confirmed in Elinor Ostrom's study of successful commons and the ways in which communities enforced the rules by which commons are governed.[2] Taken together, they show how public policy and normative institutions such as schools and workplaces can influence the trajectory of social change. The proponents of free-market thinking have known this all along. They have used the unlimited resources at their disposal to promote an ideology of competition and selfishness that reinforces a view of the world that reflects their own interests and prejudices. Hence the billions spent over decades to create think tanks, charitable foundations, mass media, university departments, and policy institutions that have made this view and these values pervasive. Their effects are toxic individualism, social breakdown, and the insulation of elites from public attitudes that would challenge their power.

> **Ostrom's rules for successfully governing commons:**
> 1. Define clear group boundaries.
> 2. Match rules governing use of common goods to local needs and conditions.
> 3. Ensure that those affected by the rules can participate in modifying the rules.
> 4. Make sure the rule-making rights of community members are respected by outside authorities.
> 5. Develop a system, carried out by community members, for monitoring members' behavior.
> 6. Use graduated sanctions for rule violators.
> 7. Provide accessible, low-cost means for dispute resolution.
> 8. Build responsibility for governing the common resource in nested tiers from the lowest level up to the entire interconnected system.[3]

Axelrod also assumes that human behavior is primarily selfish and that it is driven by rational choice. Individuals choose to co-operate because it is more successful than non-co-operation in its material rewards. We do not take this view. Even a cursory look at how people vote is enough to dispel the notion that rationality—if measured solely on the basis of material benefit—is what drives people's behavior. In real life, people are equally motivated by their values, by ideology, by their allegiance and connection to groups, by a sense of belonging, by commitment to an idea, by their sense of identity, by their attachment to place and to leaders, and by their personal sense of security. These are all powerful emotional drivers, *intrinsic* motivations that often override the *extrinsic* motivation for material reward.

Co-operation is as much a feature of human societies and personal behavior as competition. Moreover, the view that self-interest is incompatible with co-operation and the common good is deeply misleading. Given the proper context, co-operation can be more rewarding of self-interest than competition, both materially *and* psychologically. The shape and function of the institutions in which we live and work are decisive in this respect. From a system-change perspective, and the potential to change collective attitudes and behaviors, two areas are of paramount importance: the organization of social welfare and the organization of production. With the changes that are taking place in the global economy, these areas—once seen as separate domains—are becoming intimately connected. One result is that the social economy has become vital to the quality of life in market societies.

Reclaiming Social Value

The social economy has traditionally been seen as a third sector, along with the public and private sectors. But it is far more than a palliative sector at the economy's margins to help the poor and disadvantaged, as some believe. Nor is it merely a collection of social measures to remedy the failures of the free market. Rather, the social economy represents a wholly different conception of economics in which the economy serves social or collective interests, rather than those solely of private capital. It shows that markets can (and do) operate for both commercial and *non*-commercial ends. Co-operatives, commons, charitable organizations, nonprofits, and a huge range of community and social service organizations embody these values to one degree or another. Their chief common characteristic is that they produce goods and services primarily for social benefit. Most utilize some form of democratic or socially controlled governance.

The social economy continuously generates new mechanisms

for producing social value, especially in the field of human services. *Expanding the production for social value and replicating the organizational forms that embody it are key means for democratizing the state and transforming the economic paradigm of market society.*

Civil Economy and the Partner State

All political projects aim at defining and directing behavior toward some justifying social end. Typically, this has meant the conquest of political power. We aim for something different, which goes beyond the trappings of power. The challenge before us is to revive the connection between individuals in society and between human societies and the natural world. Democratizing the state—*civilizing* the state—is the necessary next stage of the democratic project.

Such a state may be called a Partner State when its aim is to serve the common good by enhancing the transformative power of civil society. The idea of the Partner State proceeds directly from the principle that in a democracy civil society is the source of political legitimacy. Strengthening civil society and reinforcing the values that build strong, solidary, and engaged communities is at the foundation of what a Partner State aims to achieve.

The decentralization of decision-making in Kerala, the enlargement of the social economy in Barcelona, and the council system of self-governance in Rojava show us how key elements of this vision are actually being applied. We can see how this applies in two areas that have come under the spotlight during the pandemic: social welfare and the elimination of work. The coronavirus has greatly accelerated the automation of production systems and the redundancy of human labor. The exponential growth of automation and artificial intelligence (AI) has in turn demanded a fundamental reappraisal of social welfare. This has important ramifications for political stability and deep implications for how we approach system change.

The reconstruction of social welfare in the time ahead has three functions. The first is to meet the social fallout from an economic system that is expelling workers from the market and making the majority of working people redundant. It is projected that fully

50 percent of the world's work activities will be automated in the next twenty years.[4] The collapse of labor as a component of capitalist production is creating a class of people, eventually constituting a social majority, whose worth will only be realized in the domain of human—not market—relations. How this is handled will ultimately determine the fate of governments and nation-states alike. This is the field of the social economy.

The second is to establish the foundations for a new kind of economy that elevates reciprocity and social value as the primary organizing principles of society. This entails the emergence of a market form that corresponds to the operations of the social economy—a social value market. The expansion and democratization of health and social care is an effective means of doing this.

The third is to reconnect people to each other and to their sense of community and common purpose. The need for security and collective welfare is universal and reaches across political, ethnic, racial, and religious divides. As economic and social insecurities grow, the need for these social goods becomes ever more acute—regardless of one's political orientation. The democratic reform of human services can be a means of social reconstruction by conjoining the common interests and collective actions of citizens across a wide spectrum of political beliefs.

All three goals are essential for a political program of deep system change. For this to succeed, we need a wholly different framework than what conventional political economy can account for—we need transition to *civil economy*.

◆ ◆ ◆

The state is more than an apparatus of collective planning or social control. It is a mechanism for collective transformation and social evolution. The state is the repository of a society's image of itself—a collective projection of an idealized common identity. It reflects the values and aspirations of those elements in society that are most able to construct this image and reinforce it through the state's institutions. Thus, a state is both real and imagined. This imagined common identity—this sense of collective belonging—is also what enables large populations to co-operate. In his book *Sapiens*, Yuval Noah Harari describes how the human capacity to create imagined orders such as myth, religion, or the nation-state enabled populations to co-operate at scale.[5] How this state is imagined, what its purpose is, and what values it embodies shape how societies evolve and how myths of collective identity transform collective ways of living and being.

Transforming the state is ultimately the long, laborious process of transforming ourselves. The deeper question is, to what purpose? What social forces will prevail? What happens when imagined orders like the American Dream, or Socialism, are no longer believed? Something must take their place.

It is now evident that in order to continue, elite rule and global inequality will require the politics of authoritarianism. Once a certain threshold of inequality is breached, only force will suffice to sustain it. We have arrived at this point. Simultaneously, a different conception of politics is manifesting itself. It is a politics of communion and the common good. At one level, it seeks to remedy the particular injustices of our current system. At a deeper level, it recognizes that the change we seek is not merely a question of outcomes—of whether a certain percentage of the population does better or worse economically or the degree to which a society has transitioned to greener forms of energy. These are the epiphenomena of a system that remains in crisis. The new political imaginary proposes a fundamental altering of social relations and a shifting of perspective from that of individual self-interest and competition to one of co-operation and common welfare.

The dire condition of the world is imposing this realization upon us. Selfishness and alienation are not only driving the material destruction of the planet. They are the source of a profound unhappiness and anxiety that has become pervasive. The grammar of living no longer makes sense. The remedy lies in human connectivity, empathy, and the rediscovery of community that comes with pursuing the common good. This entails a deepening of the democratic project—not its abandonment.

But it is not only the need for human connectivity that drives a new, deeper phase of democracy. It is also a precondition for reversing the destruction of the natural world. The concentration of wealth and inequality that plagues the globe depends on the continuing destruction of the world's ecosystems. It was the protection of oil profits that induced the fossil fuel industry to manufacture a disinformation campaign to discredit the idea of global warming—a fact they were aware of forty years ago.[6] The attack on science is an extension of this imperative to protect profits at all costs. An ecological civilization—meaning a civilization that promotes the well-being of both people *and* the planet—is not possible without dismantling the systemic inequalities and power disparities that are embedded in the capitalist paradigm and perfected in the sociopathology of the corporation.

We often hear that what is needed to move forward is a new narrative, a new story. Co-operation for our common survival is the only story. It is more than a story. It is a stark, existential fact.

The Enlightenment values of liberty, equality, and fraternity that were the foundations of the democratic ideal have not been superseded. What we know now is that those ideals are realized not through the pursuit of individual self-interest and the worship of wealth but in the humanity that is revealed when our common welfare is also our common aim. This is made possible by activating the innate capacity for connectivity and co-operation that is present in every individual and nurtures every society. To reframe Hegel's idea of a Universal Spirit revealing itself in the ontology of the state, we envision a revitalization of the human spirit in the relationships of mutuality and human empathy that flower through the creation of community. Activating those values and fostering those relationships is the new calling of politics and the cause of a Partner State.

10

FROM WELFARE STATE
TO PARTNER STATE

*It is a universal law that one cannot make oneself happy
without making others happy as well.*
— Antonio Genovesi

S INCE THE ENLIGHTENMENT, it has been assumed that the
common good is manifested through the state. By contrast, neoliberalism posited the market as the means by which the common
good is realized. Our aim has been to show that a sovereign civil
society is the true source of the common good and the surest means
of safeguarding it. Ours is an alternative vision that challenges the
primacy both of the state and the market. In the preceding chapters,
we have shown how this process involves the democratization of the
state and the empowerment of civil society from the neighborhood
level to global scale.

In this chapter, we will try and outline what this vision looks like
in practice. In the process, we will see what this means for a radically
different conception of the state and of a pathway beyond the im-
passe that is afflicting democracy in its present form.

More than mere ideas are needed to meet the urgency of the
moment. If proposals for system change are to have any relevance,
they must be strategies of connectivity, of mutuality, of social and
ecological healing. Political movements, while defending against the

predatory acts of elites, must also aim at transforming the ways in which people relate to each other and to the societies of which they are a part. This entails a transformation of those institutions—economic, social, and political—that are the matrices within which social consciousness is formed.

◆ ◆ ◆

The welfare state is arguably the greatest achievement of the democratic project to date. Despite its many imperfections, the welfare state was the fullest embodiment of the idea that the state was an instrument for the advancement of the common good. Whether to forestall an even more radical socialism or as a positive pursuit of social justice, the construction of a social safety net guaranteed by the state arose from the growing power of democratic forces in society. The rise and fall of the welfare state may be taken as a barometer of the democratic pressure to advance the collective welfare. The appropriation of public goods by capital as described in chapter one marks the decline of democratic values and the power of civil and political institutions to defend them. This in turn, triggers the crisis of legitimacy that now bedevils the liberal state.

If politics is to play a transformative role, the question of social welfare is both critical and strategic. It is in the arena of social welfare that the political values of a democratic civil society overlap most with the claims to legitimacy of the state. The recovery of social welfare as the central mission of the state does not mean a return to the paternalism of the past. For all the benefits that the welfare state brought to public health and welfare, it is easy to forget the deficiencies that came with it. A host of new problems presented themselves. The bureaucratization of care pitted the inflexible demands of centralized management systems against the individual needs of citizens and communities. State welfare presupposed personal powerlessness—and poverty. Social welfare was stigmatized. The human and social components of care were all but erased.

How social welfare evolves in the coming period will profoundly influence the course of political events in all countries, rich and poor.

The integrated nature of systemic crises, from global warming to mass unemployment, guarantees this. A progressive strategy that addresses the need for new political forms and for rebuilding connectivity means looking to a new kind of governance that goes beyond representative democracy and embodies a *relational theory of change*. The significance of social welfare for politics lies in its potential for rebuilding trust, connectivity, and solidarity across political, religious, and ideological divides.

The concept of the Partner State was first theorized by Cosma Orsi, in his exploration of the Political Economy of Solidarity.[1] It was further elaborated by Vasilis Kostakis in relation to the commons[2] and later in Ecuador during the course of a research project exploring how the principles of peer production and the commons could transition the Ecuadorian economy away from its dependence on resource extraction. Free and open access to knowledge was a key thrust of this effort, in which I took part.[3,4] Peer production refers to a way of producing goods and services through self-organizing networks of individuals that share both in the production and the benefits generated by these goods, particularly through the use of the Internet. We cited one such example of commons-based peer production in the collaborative design and manufacture of emergency ventilators in chapter eight. As a collective and egalitarian form of value creation, Michel Bauwens has described peer production as the "socialism of the 21st Century."[5]

One formulation of the Partner State has to do with this commons-based transformation of production systems.[6] Our approach has focused on the transformation of social and political relations and the role of civil power in this process. In both cases, the role of the state is centered on maximizing co-operation and the commons as foundational principles for a new social/political paradigm.

In modern times, the regulatory role of the state has habitually swung from the promotion of either the private sector through support of the capitalist economy or the redistributive function of government through state control of economic planning. The first submits the public and social economies to the requirements of capital. The second submits the capitalist and social economies to the needs of centralized state planning. Both models have come at unsustainably high economic and social costs. And while there have been varieties of these two models, mostly in some combination of public and private dominance, there has never been an instance in which the needs of civil society and the values of the social economy have predominated in the state's management of economic and social policy. What is missing is the incorporation of reciprocity as a factor in the creation not only of social value but also of economic value. In theory and practice, the Partner State is the first state formation to do this. This, in turn, requires an entirely new framework for what we understand as political economy.

The Partner State is above all an *enabling* state. It maximizes the capacity of civil society to create social value through co-operation and to act as the *primary agent* in the formation of public policy. Citizens, acting through civil institutions that they control, directly influence the direction and execution of public policy. However, the enabling role of the state is not confined to the promotion of social value. It enlarges the scope for both personal and social development *beyond market relations*. It safeguards open access to the economy. It provides space for many models of entrepreneurship, including collective and commons-based forms of enterprise such as co-operatives and peer-to-peer networks. It does so by incorporating the principle of reciprocity within the operating structures of the market economy.

How, then, would such a system actually work?

The state has the capacity to be a synthesizer and facilitator, to set the rules and provide a flow of core funds that allows an economy of social value creation to flourish. It has the capacity to organize large projects, and at national scales. It represents the general interest. The social economy is a space of interpersonal and productive democracy in contrast to the state's representative and deliberative democracy. In a very real sense, the two domains manifest the requirements of collective versus personal citizenship, and each is the necessary complement to the other. A new social contract must be based on a framework that synthesizes the regulatory, redistributive, and representative attributes of government with the social, moral, and relational elements of civil society as a whole. This includes the humanization of the economy through the incorporation of civil values. This framework is captured in the idea of civil economy. It is the philosophical underpinning of the Partner State.

The Return of Civil Economy

At the outset of our discussion, we traced the evolution of the idea of civil society and its connection to theories of social, economic, and political organization. One tradition—that of Adam Smith— conceived of political economy as a social regime in which the market operates autonomously of moral, social, or interpersonal considerations. The second tradition, lost from historical view but re-emerging in the context of the current crisis of economics, is the civil economy tradition of Antonio Genovesi. For Genovesi, economic life is an extension of social life and incorporates all those social, moral, and relational elements that are also at the foundation of community.

Civil economy is the regime that sees society, economics, and politics as an integrated whole whose ultimate purpose is the promotion of social well-being and public happiness. In a fundamental way, the case studies we have been discussing and the movements for system change that we have described are attempts to incorporate the social and the relational back into the operations of market society and our systems of governance. This is not possible within the traditional formulation of political economy, which isolates the social from the economic on the one hand and from the state on the other. What is missing is the recognition that human sociality as expressed through reciprocity and the practice of co-operation is to be lived not only in the personal sphere of family, friendship, and communal life but also in the operations of civil governance and the economy itself. The market, too, is a space where fraternity and the advancement of mutual benefit can thrive.

Stefano Zamagni put it very eloquently:

> Civil economy proposes a multifaceted humanism whereby the market is not opposed or "controlled," but is seen as a civil arena on a par with others, that is, as one aspect of the public sphere; as something that if conceived and experienced as an environment open also to the principles of reciprocity and gratuitousness, can contribute towards the construction of a *civitas*—the body of citizens comprising the state.[7]

This is what we are aiming at.

The Partner State enlarges the scope of personal autonomy and liberty while reinforcing the social bonds that build healthy communities and a vibrant civil society. Like the examples of Spain, Kerala, and Rojava, the Partner State establishes the sovereignty of civil society by democratizing and decentralizing the institutions of governance. This process can begin most effectively with the democratization of the institutions and services already provided by the state—especially with respect to the provision of social care and human services. But it also applies to the democratization and humanization of the economy.

In the face of massive social dislocation, social care is very clearly one area where radical reform is a priority. But for this to be meaningful, we must first understand the nature of social care. Social care is what economists call a *relational good*—a good or a service that is embedded in an actual relationship between *persons* and whose production depends on the *conjoined action* of the parties. Unlike standard goods, which decrease in value with their use, the value of relational goods increases with use. Education is a good example. It takes both the teacher *and* the student(s) investing the time, attention, and effort to make learning possible. The more they engage, the greater the value of the outcome. Another example is the collective joy and excitement that is created when a crowd is enjoying a football game in a stadium. It is a relational experience that cannot be created on one's own. Friendship is a relational good. Finally, relational assets, such as friendship, share many characteristics with civic virtues: their value increases with use and declines with nonuse.[8]

In social care, as in friendship, it is the quality of the relationship *itself* that carries value. Relational goods acquire value through sincerity, or *genuineness*; they cannot be bought or sold or merely consumed as impersonal services. In the welfare state, the relational quality of care was eclipsed, as was the agency and individuality of the person who received it. The human connection was replaced by the corporate administration of services to anonymous subjects that were deprived of any power or control over the services they received. State welfare programs became a means of surveillance and control over a vast underclass.

The state-directed command and control model of care is a relic of the industrial machine society. It replicates the management systems—and class attitudes—of that era. And while universal programs of social welfare greatly enhanced the security of citizens, they also displaced the traditional bonds of mutual help that underlay previous communal models of care that were provided by family, friends, mutual help societies, and other forms of communal care from time immemorial. The mass scale of the deprivation and dependence that came with the transition to a market society far surpassed the capacities of communal care systems.

This process of social precariousness has accelerated. Over the last decade, working people have experienced a squeeze on wages greater than at any time in the preceding 150 years.[9] Labor market deregulation, the assault on unions, and advances in automation now pose unprecedented risks to everyone who depends on a wage. The decline of consumer buying power because of precarity, low wages, and systemic unemployment undermines the very basis of the capitalist economy.

The model is unfeasible. The old paradigm of social welfare directed to the poor and unemployed in an economy based on human wage labor has been superseded. Rising precarity demands a response. We can replicate the paternalistic systems of the past, or we can look for alternatives that actually grapple with the unprecedented changes now underway.

Unlike previous times when social welfare focused on repairing the social wreckage of the capitalist system, social welfare in our time has an even greater role to play. Instead of providing relief to the casualties of an unjust system, an expanded understanding of social welfare may be the cornerstone for a new kind of economic system altogether. The current trajectory of capitalism is not only unsustainable, it is politically, socially, and morally bankrupt. Its casualties are not merely the unlucky individuals of a growing underclass. The elevation of profit above all other values is undoing the very fabric of society itself. The social alienation, the toxic individualism, the collapse of trust, the death of culture, the epidemic of depression, and the dissolution of the communal sense may be traced to the capitalist destruction of social value.

Social care and the co-operative values that underpin the social economy are the foundations from which a broken and unmoored society might be rebuilt to serve authentic human needs. The reconstruction of social welfare is one means of building a new kind of polity by pursuing a program of social reformation.

Important innovations in democratic governance have redefined the role of the state in the area of social welfare. Much of this effort has been directed to the reform of social care itself, by returning it to the control of citizens and the community. Instead of treating care as a commodity and a source of profit—the route of privatization— social care is being redefined on the basis of its human and communal value, beyond the reach of market forces. The democratization of social care realigns the roles of state and civil society within a larger framework of social and political transformation. Social co-operatives are a prime example of how co-operative values are rehumanizing social care by restoring the social and interpersonal relations that are its foundation.

Social Co-ops

Social co-ops emerged in Italy in the late seventies following the deinstitutionalization of psychiatric patients and the dissatisfaction of caregivers and families with the quality of care provided by the state. Caregivers teamed up with families to create social care programs that were owned and operated by frontline workers and the people they served. The earliest social co-ops were typically concerned with the provision of support to people with disabilities. The resources, leadership, and collective experience of Italy's co-operative movement—among the largest and most sophisticated in Europe—aided these efforts.

Today, there are more than 14,000 social co-ops employing 380,000 people across Italy. In 2015, social co-ops generated over 8.1 billion euros in economic value. While comprising only 20 percent of the nonprofit sector, social co-ops generate more than 40 percent of its economic turnover.[10] In the city of Bologna, 85 percent of health and social care programs are delivered by social co-operatives, providing a vast array of services under contract to municipal and public authorities. Social co-ops provide treatment for substance users, retrain and employ ex-prisoners, provide travel and recreation services to families of disabled people, create new community services for children and families, and provide long-term care to the elderly.

Social co-ops have been at the forefront of democratizing public services in Italy and offered a social alternative to privatization. They show how democratic user control can be the basis for a system of care that is founded on the collective production of social value, not through centralized control, or as a form of charity, or for private profit. Social co-ops mobilized the principles of the social economy to reconstruct the entire edifice of health and social welfare.

But the model is not without its problems. Chief among these is the reliance on sympathetic governments and public contracts—many of which replicate the market thinking and cost-cutting priorities of private providers. Capitalist market logic has become pervasive not only among politicians. Over the years, it has also dominated the thinking of co-operative leaders who have lost touch with the founding principles of the co-operative movement itself. The pressure to conform to the business logic of the free market highlights both how difficult and how necessary is the struggle to practice economics according to other measures of value. Co-operatives are navigating at the crosscurrents of these opposing forces.

In the system of social co-ops described above, while the design and delivery of social care is in the hands of care workers and end-users, the economic basis of the model is still rooted in the capitalist system and the legislative support of the state. The payment of these services still comes from the transfer of tax dollars by the state or from the payments of individual users, which are based in turn on wages earned in the wider economy. It is a form of co-operative social democracy. Social co-ops are thus dependent on public contracts, tax dollars, and a market economy over which they have no control. This is equally true of the social economy as a whole.

Like the social economy, social co-ops are vulnerable to changes in public policy and government priorities and to the colonizing and profit-seeking aims of capital. What is needed for such a model to thrive—beyond progressive public policy—is an autonomous market that corresponds to the communal values of the social economy and is capable of supporting its operations. Moreover, it is not possible to advance a coherent theory of the social economy without a corresponding theory of a social *market* that provides the social economy with an economic foundation. Without a social market that replicates and reflects the values and operations of the entities that comprise it, the social economy remains a vaporous and half-realized idea.

The Social Value Market

The creation of a true social market is of paramount importance for the generation of social value and for establishing the autonomy and economic independence of the social economy itself. Without it, the social economy will always be dependent on government or private capital and the emergence of a Partner State would not be possible.

What, then, *is* a social value market?

Just as a commercial market makes possible the types of production and exchange relations that generate surplus value (profit), a social market fosters social relationships for the provision of services to people. As opposed to the production of goods and services for their commercial value, social markets sustain the production of *relational goods* for social value. These kinds of co-operative relationships, based on reciprocity and mutual benefit, are the bedrock of the social economy. We can appreciate the enormous relevance of this social mechanism by looking at the work of Fureai Kippu.

Fureai Kippu

Fureai Kippu is a co-operative system providing care to seniors in Japan. The term *Fureai Kippu* means "ticket for a caring relationship" and refers to the ticket or credit that is earned when one volunteers their time helping seniors. It is a time-bank system where members can earn time credits or points for the hours they volunteer providing physical care, home help, personal services, and emotional assistance to other, care-dependent, members. These credits are then registered by their co-op as a form of electronic currency and saved in their personal accounts. It works on the same principle as an air miles plan. Time credit holders can withdraw and use their credits to access care for themselves or relatives as required. The system is composed of a network of local co-operatives that track and then reimburse volunteer time on the basis of these earned credits. Credits can also be sent to other locales where the services can be redeemed to serve friends or loved ones there. Fureai Kippu has branches in San Francisco, LA, and cities in Europe.

When the system was first created in 1995, it operated primarily as an autonomous community-based network of co-operating volunteers. Since then, the model has become a key complement to the state care systems, and governments at both local and federal levels have actively supported it. Yokohama City near Tokyo successfully recruited thousands of volunteers into the system by modifying the scheme to allow members to exchange time credits for services other than elder care. Young parents, for example, can use credits to pay for childcare or other services.

The quality of real caring relationships that Fureai Kippu has fostered among people who live in the same community creates a level of trust in the system that far exceeds the services provided by the state. It has also strengthened the social bonds—the social capital—that are the foundation of caring communities. Surveys in Japan found that most recipients preferred Fureai Kippu care providers over those paid in cash.[11] The relationships and the level of care received were said to be qualitatively different. According to the testimony of members, Fureai Kippu created for them a personal connection and a sense of reciprocity unmatched by traditional payment systems. When a network member provides a service, the person being cared for often becomes an extension of the member's family.

Just as importantly, many of those who receive care valued the fact that they too can contribute to the system and to the care of others. The reciprocity inherent in the model equalizes power relationships and changes the social dynamic between caregiver and recipient. The recipient is neither a supplicant nor a client, but a participant in a social nexus that produces care as a common social good—not a state benefit or a commercial service, or a form of charity.

Fureai Kippu shows that reciprocity and mutualism can be valuated in social as opposed to monetary terms. The model shows how a reciprocity-based system of community-controlled co-ops can work with state systems to offer an alternative to the privatization of what should remain *social* relationships of caring. The localized control that communities can exercise over their care through these co-operatives and the presence of public policies to support them are key for the cultivation of a caring society. This re-embeds caring relationships inside communities in a way that bureaucratized state systems or for-profit models never can. We can now imagine how a time-bank system could be adapted to support and expand this kind of social value and how it might be applied across the entire field of health and social care. It's a question of design and political vision.

But I wish to be very clear that this does not mean the elimination of universal programs such as public health insurance, or pensions, or unemployment benefits. There is a reason why universal centrally administered programs are so valued. They safeguard the principle of equality in the access of public goods. Such universal programs rely on the pooled resources of society as a whole to finance and a comprehensive administration system to manage. The democratization of care does not absolve the state from its responsibility as a steward of public welfare. But if these systems are reimagined as forms of public commonwealth, and if citizens have control rights in the form of voting shares in a co-operative system, they could neither be revoked nor sold off without the knowledge and consent of the citizenry. Distributed control rights and democratic accountability can reclaim the commonwealth of a society and safeguard it for posterity. Democratization constrains the state to serve the common welfare. What is true of public services is also true of material goods such as natural resources and energy systems, as well as immaterial goods such as knowledge, culture, and information.

Fureai Kippu creates a social market for the production and exchange of social value. It shows how an alternative value-system can be the basis for a new kind of market—a new kind of *economy*—if the institutions are in place to give it form and effect. The credit that is earned by helping others is a form of social currency based on reciprocity. It works because people accept and stand behind its value. This, in turn, is based on the mutual trust that has been established by a specific community of users. In Fureai Kippu, reciprocity is amplified and rewarded, resulting in a virtuous cycle of pro-social behavior. It is not only individuals that benefit; society as a whole benefits through the increase in social capital and mutual trust that is generated.

This is not an abstraction. In the context of extreme social polarization, it is only through the creation of direct, mutually beneficial relationships that arise from co-operation in a shared undertaking that bridges are built across social and political divides. Whether you label yourself as progressive or conservative, working in reciprocity with others for a common benefit changes your perception of those who, in other contexts, you might perceive as antagonists. This is one of the great and underappreciated strengths of co-operatives. They establish common cause among their members despite the diversity of views they may hold.

Can such a system be scaled to establish a body of goods and services not only for social welfare but also for the wider economy?

If helping others or engaging in socially valuable work such as public health, protecting the environment, or participating in public works can be translated into exchangeable social value, there is the basis for establishing a new economic setup in which a social value system operates independently of capitalist market relations. The difference between the two is the distinction between the production of commodities for profit and the generation of human behaviors for social benefit. One is aimed at the promotion of personal gain, the other at the promotion of a common good.

All of this, of course, depends on whether such a system can be made economically viable. There are at least three means of establishing the viability of this system. One is through the autonomous production of social value mediated through a social market as outlined above. In this approach, we can imagine a setup in which social economy organizations are listed on a social value exchange where citizens can contribute capital—much like the open co-operative model used to finance co-ops in Rojava. Instead of a financial return on their investment, citizen contributions are translated into human services. One can thus imagine a social value exchange operating as an investment and clearing mechanism for social value.

A second approach rests on an understanding that the social economy is continuous with the public economy insofar as its wider social aims are concerned. This is the case with the social co-operative movement and the co-operative economy more generally in Italy. The state formally acknowledges the social value of co-operatives, and its obligation to support them is written into the Italian constitution. This alignment of the social and public economies is a foundational principle of the Partner State. Public support for social economy enterprises through the tax system, or the creation of dedicated social investment funds, is merely an extension of this principle.

The third approach is the redistribution of wealth and the democratization of the production process within the wider economy.

The appropriation of hoarded wealth from national oligarchies is one obvious target, as are taxation of the rich and the elimination of inherited wealth and privilege.

A further element for the evolution of social markets is the provision of a universal citizen's income as a basic right of citizenship. This would in turn allow individuals to devote a portion of their time to the production of goods and services for social benefit. It is also the means by which cultural wealth—such as fine art, music, craftsmanship, and the creation of knowledge—can be sustained and offer a viable means of livelihood to creatives, independently of the commercial market.

A citizen's income, financed by returning tax rates to those operating in the 1950s and 60s (upwards of 47 percent for corporations), the taxing of capital gains, the taxation of wealth as well as income, and the elimination of tax loopholes and offshore tax havens, could easily finance a universal basic income. A citizen's income is one way of establishing a financial floor for the operation of a co-operative commonwealth by redistributing wealth and eliminating the insecurity and precarity that stalks citizens in market societies the world over.

◆ ◆ ◆

The failures of privatization have given rise to calls for the renationalization of public goods and services ranging from water to data systems and railways. This represents a regression to planned economy models that take no account of the need for less, not greater, centralization and the need for greater, not less, citizen control and accountability. An alternative path starts from the redesign of public services and public wealth to fully integrate control rights for citizens.

These kinds of changes depend on the capacity of a society's members to influence the behavior of their governments as active partners and participants in the design and delivery of the goods and services they use. Transition to democratization at this level involves broad-based political mobilization at a scale that has not been seen in generations. Unlike previous eras, the centers of political control and economic power are no longer localized in individual nation-states—they are transnational and global, and their collective impact and reach is unprecedented.

Political struggle and the transition to new forms of collective democracy must therefore occur at multiple levels simultaneously: at the level of neighborhoods and municipalities where people live and work, at the level of nations and national governments where people's collective identities operate, and at the global level of international networks and power circuits that ultimately determine the trajectory of political and economic development.

The evolution of transnational networks that embody a new paradigm of social and economic development is already far advanced. The fair trade movement pioneered this approach by focusing on behavioral change and reworking established patterns of production and consumption. La Via Campesina and the multitudes that are engaged in the global struggle against climate change and environmental destruction are also emblematic of this emergent glocalism.

The transformative potential of online communities that utilize co-operative and commons systems for the production and sharing of knowledge and other immaterial goods is a new modality altogether. This, too, is an area where the Partner State has a central role to play. The emergence of commons-based knowledge systems and exchange platforms that link global information with localized production systems is a new production modality that integrates global information systems with co-operative and commons logic.[12]

The use of digital communications for political mobilization, for raising awareness, and for equalizing the hierarchical relations of power that characterize capitalist production systems is establishing a new mechanism for radically altering existing political and economic relations. The vision of politics as the expression of a new collectivity oriented around the common good is already visible and present. It is at work as much in the online tools of Decidim in Barcelona as in the council system of Democratic confederalism in Rojava.

All these movements share a revisioning of state institutions. They also require the creation of autonomous civil institutions that allow society to play the partnering role that this democratization process requires. Civil institutions that can mobilize civil society in the management of public affairs are the counterpoint to democratizing and civilizing the state. In the case of Rojava, this is the organizing role played by TEV-DEM. In Spain, it is the engagement of civil organizations that inherited the activist mantle of the *Indignados*. In Kerala, it has been the civil structures embedded in civil empowerment and propelled by an activist civil society in partnership with the state.

Without the countervailing power of an organized and active civil society exercising control rights in the commanding institutions of social and economic life, no effort at democratizing the state will endure for long.

11

CIVILIZING THE STATE: PRINCIPLES AND POLICIES

THE NEED FOR A "NEXT SYSTEM" is no longer a moral imperative with respect to social justice. This has been true from the dawn of civilization. Human societies have always had to defend against the predatory instincts of those seeking to control and monopolize the means of life. Today, it is an existential imperative. Unless civil societies create the means to democratize governance and economies, to civilize the state by fully incorporating the civil values and common aims that are the source of its legitimacy, neither politics nor economics will solve our collective human dilemma. The real issue is whether, and how, this systemic shift might come about.

Over the course of the preceding chapters, we have seen how popular movements, as well as governments, have envisioned a set of ideas and principles that reframe the roles and responsibilities of state and citizenry toward a more inclusive, more participatory form of governance in pursuit of the common good as the primary goal of government.

These principles, taken together, form a new framework for imagining state and civil society as a symbiotic partnership whose center of gravity is neither the market nor the state but society itself, organized to perfect the practice of democracy and reciprocity as the mechanism for both personal and social well-being. The idea of the Partner State we are exploring here is based on these principles, which may be summarized as follows:

+ That the purpose of the state is to pursue and defend the common good.
+ That the legitimacy of the state derives from a free and sovereign civil society.
+ That civil society is distinct from, and pre-eminent to, its systems of governance.
+ That the common good is achieved through the continuous empowerment and activation of civil society.
+ That citizenship is based on acceptance of, and participation in, democratic practice.
+ That the political and economic order is based on the production of social value and the maximal distribution of democratic practice.
+ That governance is shared through direct, decentralized, and deliberative democracy.
+ That political democracy is inseparable from economic democracy.
+ That capital and markets are subject to social control and in service of social, as well as individual, aims.
+ That a universal commonwealth is essential to the common good.
+ That individual well-being is a function of communal well-being.
+ That human society is continuous with the natural world and dependent on a healthy biosphere.
+ That co-operation, mutuality, and social justice are the means to economic, political, and social advancement.

The dilution of corporate power and the democratization of the economy is the vital next phase of democratization, completing at long last the incorporation of the democratic principle throughout the body politic and ending its confinement to the rituals of representative government.

On Corporations

The question of social controls over the size and influence of corporate power in market society has a long history. Let us take the U.S. as an example. Beginning in the late 1800s, the rise of monopolies in key sectors of the American economy prompted a concerted effort on the part of government to prevent the control of markets by corporations and to protect the principle of free competition in the economy. This was especially true in essential sectors such as rail and transport, oil, coal, banking, telecommunications, and agriculture. A series of federal antitrust laws were passed to break up monopolies and preserve the freedom of Americans to build businesses and to participate in economic life. Indeed, antitrust laws were regarded by the Supreme Court as a "charter of freedom" designed to protect free enterprise in America. As stated by Senator John Sherman, author of the landmark Sherman Antitrust Act of 1890, "If we will not endure a king as a political power, we should not endure a king over the production, transportation, and sale of any of the necessaries of life."[1]

The act passed unanimously, and even more noteworthy is the fact that Sherman was himself a Republican.

Today, the relevance of measures for reducing corporate control of markets—and also of politics—is clear. What is far less evident is whether the kinds of measures that were adopted in the late 19th century to curtail the rise of cartels is feasible in today's political environment. Things have changed. Today's Republicans and conservatives are a different breed than their forebearers. With the passage of decisions such as Citizen's United by the U.S. Supreme Court and the domination of corporate interests in all branches of government, it is doubtful whether even existing statutes could be enforced to limit corporate power in the economy.

But we are speaking of what something like a Partner State requires for the kind of paradigm change we are proposing. The application of anti-monopoly legislation to limit the size and influence of capital is crucial. It is a prerequisite for a pluralist economy where markets are accessible to all, and where co-operative and collective forms of enterprise comprise a significant part of society's productive capacity. This, in turn, requires a mechanism for democratizing and distributing the accumulated wealth and organizational resources of large corporations and for diversifying the private sector. There are a number of ways to accomplish this, for example:

+ Enterprises over a certain size (say 700 employees) or controlling more than a maximum allowable percentage of a market would have to divest and subdivide into separate enterprises.

+ The ownership of subdivided enterprises must first be offered to employees as a form of worker co-operative as a right of first refusal.

+ No enterprise may be sold to a third party or apply for bankruptcy without first being offered for purchase to its employees.

+ All enterprises, regardless of their structure, would be required to set aside a portion of their profits in a common trust to be used to finance possible subdivision of the enterprise and transition to worker ownership.

+ All enterprises must devote a percentage of their profit in support of the social economy.

+ All enterprises must operate in accordance with provisions that clearly account for the impact of their operations on both the natural and the social environment. Negative impacts must be identified through compulsory social and environmental audits and their costs incorporated and covered by the operations of the enterprise. Enterprises unable to do this would be subject to fines or closure.

Such measures would not only minimize the domination of one enterprise model. They would also establish a regime in which employees gradually become owners and shareholders of the enterprises in which they work. Wealth would be distributed more fairly among those who contribute to its creation, and the ability of individual entrepreneurs and private businesses to participate in the economy would be strengthened by a more equal playing field in a framework of social and environmental constraints.

On Money and Investment

If economic democracy is the basis for an alternative to capitalism, the linchpin to system change is social control over capital. Nowhere is this more urgent than in social control over the creation of money and the management of investment for public benefit.

When the Bank of England disclosed in 2014 that the creation of money in modern economies was through the creation of new debt by commercial banks, most people had no idea.[2] Most still believed that banks issue new loans by lending out the money they receive from deposits. In fact, the reverse is true. Banks create money in the form of new loans, expressed as deposits, which are then circulated as currency by the recipient. Whenever a bank makes a loan, including to government, it simultaneously creates a matching deposit in the borrower's bank account, thereby creating new money.

This means that the mere *creation* of money, as opposed to functioning as a public service to provide a means of exchange for the economy, is in reality an endless source of wealth delivered to the owners of private banks through the interest that is charged on these loans. Governments, individuals, and enterprises are all subjected to this system, which in turn drives the massive accumulation of unearned wealth by the one percent, the skyrocketing indebtedness of the population, and the chronic underfunding of public investments by the state. As Thomas Picketty has shown, this system is the primary source of wealth inequality in our societies.[3]

It need not be so. Money can be conceived as a public good. The creation of publicly owned banks that are responsible for the generation of debt-free money as a public resource has been tested and was for many years the operating model for the Bank of Canada. From 1935 to 1974, the Bank of Canada created interest-free money that was used by the Government of Canada to finance major infrastructure projects in the country. Interest-free financing paid for the construction of the St. Lawrence Seaway, the Welland Canal, the Trans-Canada Highway, public housing, and a broad range of social programs including financial aid for veterans to attend university and to acquire farmland, and the development of the federal health care system including the Canada Pension Plan and Medicare.

Other examples of publicly owned banks include the Reconstruction Finance Corporation in the U.S. (1932–1957) that financed the recovery of American banking and business during the Great Depression and the New Deal, the Central Bank of New Zealand, Kreditanstalt für Wiederaufbau (KfW) in Germany, and the Bank of North Dakota.

If governments today are steeped in debt and unable to invest in public services and the rebuilding of public infrastructure, it is largely because they borrow their money from private banks at interest. The reintroduction of public banks as the source of money creation and the financing of public spending is fundamental to exerting social control over capital and the financial sector. Conceived as a public utility, a central public bank can treat money as an essential public resource for the operation of a healthy economy and the promotion of public benefit.

This does not preclude the operation of other forms of lending institution. Private banks could continue to provide loans for the financing of private ventures. They would occupy a specific niche in the private capital market. In addition to supplying private banks with currency at interest—*precisely the opposite of what happens now*—a central public bank would be a key source of investment capital not only for the social economy but also for the public economy and the operations of the state.

Other forms of co-operative and social financing could also be supported with preferential tax and public policies to encourage the growth of financial institutions that are owned and controlled by their users and by local communities. Credit unions are the prime example of this, as are community capital organizations that provide investment and development capital for local economic development, new business start-ups, and the financing of social economy projects and enterprises.

A transformative monetary policy would promote the democratization of capital at all levels, including the use of locally generated forms of community and co-operative capital to promote local development and to extend the conscious use of capital as a public resource for the advancement of common economic benefits.

The proposals outlined above are hardly comprehensive. However, the principles that animate them frame an understanding of the human condition that carries beyond the narrow, and ultimately artificial, precepts of traditional political economy and advance the democratic project bequeathed to us by those who came before. Much as these principles are rooted in the social evolution of our species, and central to its survival, it is through the cultivation of our common humanity and the solidary bonds of fraternity and mutuality that they are made real in the politics we choose.

EPILOGUE

W E HAVE SPOKEN of the need to reclaim politics and to reframe its purpose. Ultimately, practicing politics is an act of
faith. It is the conviction that one's choices are meaningful and that
one's actions matter. Practicing politics assumes that the patterns of
our collective life are not fixed, that societies evolve, and that we have
a role to play in determining the direction and purpose of this evolution. Set against the great weight of hierarchy and elite rule that
marks the vast bulk of human experience—past and present—politics is a revolt against the gods of entrenched power and privilege.
Politics as we have discussed it, and democracy in particular, tames
power and makes it the currency of our collective life—not merely
the plaything of privilege. It is a wholly revolutionary conception of
human affairs and entirely unwelcomed by those whose privileges
rest on stasis and the perpetuation of things as they are, not as they
might be.

We started our discussion with Aristotle and his conception of
human nature as essentially social, that the individual can realize
his or her life's purpose only in the company and companionship of
others. More than this, politics extends beyond the individual and
concerns the happiness and well-being of the whole of a community
not just a segment; its ultimate aim and purpose is the common
good. The legitimacy of government, and of the state itself, rests on
the degree to which this common purpose is served. In turn, the

common good can only be achieved through the active involvement of the whole of a political community, what Aristotle termed civil society.

I have proposed that human societies must always contend with the tensions of co-operation versus competition, of the conflict between the predatory behavior of elites and the need of every society to protect itself from this predation. Democracy, I have argued, is the prime tool of social self-defence. Nor is there an end to this process.

People have always dreamed about what kind of utopia best serves our conception of the good society. From the Kingdom of Heaven to the Marxist idea of a classless society to the technocratic fantasies of Silicon Valley, such visions are not merely metaphorical. They embody paramount ideals that mold the culture and conduct of whole societies. Today, such utopias seem in short supply. Perhaps it is a measure of a wider disenchantment with ideals as such. So far as progressive movements are concerned—those aiming at social justice—the dreams have been atomized. The politics of identity have eclipsed the collective social sense of the left. Identity politics embody the sense of grievance and defeat that characterise the perceived failure of the socialist project and internalize the individualism and self-obsession that are the hallmarks of the neoliberal era. Solidarity around a shared social struggle has given way to solipsism. Meanwhile, on the right, the traditional concern with established moral values, property rights, social stability, low taxes, and small government has devolved into the naked pursuit of power—regardless of cost—and nativist privilege parading as patriotism. What was once a coherent body of conservative values and ideas is now pure reaction.

In the U.S., this has morphed into a kind of populist political trance wholly removed from reality. The suggestibility of such a movement, coupled with the suspension of critical reason and fealty to a demagogue who knows neither shame nor limits, is beyond frightening. These are the signs of a democracy that has failed its members, lost their trust, and neglected to cultivate in them the civic skills and attitudes that might have forestalled such a failure. It is not our better angels but the darker demons of our nature that are now called forth to seek retribution. This is Trump's true appeal—his calling to our worst selves—and the source of his power.

Elsewhere, the sense of betrayal by citizens has engendered a crisis of legitimacy that is global. Set against the challenges of inequality, environmental destruction, and climate change, humanity is at an inflection point. But now, as never before, the human community confronts these challenges consciously, as interdependent phenomena. The connections have been made clear. This in itself assigns a new frame for our understanding and sets a new stage for our action. How we act collectively and the forms of governance we create, both where we live and globally, will determine whether the democratic promise will prevail and, by extension, whether the challenges we face as a species will be met.

Throughout our narrative, we have seen how the problems of collective governance are continuously evolving solutions that extend the practice of politics not only to civilize the state but, even more profoundly, to reinforce the innate sociability of people through the expansion of co-operation and the practice of democracy in everyday life. It is no surprise that these very practices, and the values that sustain them, are under threat. Not since the revolutionary movements of the mid-1800s has such a groundswell of mass mobilizations emerged to complete the promise of the democratic project. What is so striking today is how the politics we choose is linked to the ecological imperative of human survival. We are in the midst of a great social schism, a growing polarization between political regression and political rebirth, and we face the difficult task of bridging opposing forces with a vision that is equal to the challenges we face in common. Co-operation in pursuit of the common good must be at the heart of this vision.

What this vision looks like in practice is not a mystery. The stories we have set out in these pages offer us real-world cases of a future reimagined and from whose examples we might learn and be inspired. From the progressive municipalism of Barcelona to the decentralism and civil mobilizations of Kerala and the stateless democracy of Rojava, we have seen how inventive and various are the forms such a vision can take. Yet its principles of co-operation, pluralism, mutual benefit, democratic accountability, and concern for the collective welfare remain constant. The state, deriving its legitimacy from the pursuit of the common good, has a central role to play in the furtherance of these values. Nor must these values be bound by the state form as we have known it. The Democratic Confederalism of Rojava is an object lesson in the possibilities of a communitarian civil democracy that is stateless.

Our concept of the Partner State draws heavily from these experiences. It is one way of articulating a form of civil economy that embodies the co-operative and communitarian principles that might civilize states and humanize economies.

Meanwhile, the great questions of global inequality, dispossession, the destruction of commons, the right to a dignified livelihood, and the regeneration of the earth as championed by the peasants and Indigenous people of La Via Campesina remain central to global struggle. They have bonded allies across class, ethnicity, and national boundaries. The struggles are intensifying, and the momentum for change is accelerating.

As I write these lines, large things are happening in India. Peasants from the states of Punjab and Haryana have abandoned their farms and gathered in the hundreds of thousands on the outskirts of Delhi. Living in their tractors and trucks, they are fighting for the repeal of legislation that they fear will destroy their livelihoods.

The march on Delhi followed the staging of the largest general strike in human history. In a staggering display of civil solidarity, 250 million workers and farmers took part in the strike, a quarter of all working people in India. Five states—Kerala, Puducherry, Odisha, Assam, and Telangana—were completely shut down. The strike saw work stoppages in banks, financial services, government offices, transport, steel production, ports and docks, telecommunication services, plantations, power generating units, coal mines, oil and natural gas production, and millions of other workplaces, large and small. The target of the strikers is the far-right regime of Narendra Modi and his collusion with multinationals to end market protections for India's farmers. A way of life hangs in the balance.

In Delhi, Modi is not backing down, and the farmers are not leaving. So far, at least 248 people have been killed. Despite the pandemic, massive economic hardship, and unemployment at 27 percent, the movement is vowing to extend the protests through the summer and across the country. It is one more front, one more fault line in the global order of capital.

◆　◆　◆

It is in times of crisis and impending collapse that ruling elites are most dangerous. The viciousness with which their interests will be protected is proportional to the threat presented by real prospects for change.

Tragically, it appears that a kind of siege mentality has taken hold of global elites. We are in the age of the global gated community. The rich are so insulated from the grim realities that they are quite prepared to let the world burn beyond their gates. It is entirely likely that system change will come not from peaceful efforts at transition but from the implosion of the global capitalist system, prompted by a convergence of social, economic, and environmental crises. If the question then, is "what follows," the answer lies in the seeds that have been sown all around us. The examples examined in this book are a possible future taking shape in the womb of the present.

Those of us working for a new vision must be oriented around two outcomes. One aim is to create system change within the institutions of the present system. The focus here is on shifting political structures, public policies, power relations, and the narrative of our collective worldview. Political organizing on a massive scale and the emergence of something like a Partner State can be one result. It will be propelled by the natural human impulse for social justice. Human solidarity, co-operation, and devotion to the common good are its foundations. Popular mobilization and the gathering strength of solidarity across borders and cultures are its expressions.

The other aim is the creation in situ of those models of politics, economics, and community that embody a new vision and carry it forward regardless of the wider political environment. This, too, is a continuous process. And we live in extraordinary times. Small movements have far reaching effects. It's as the chemist and Nobel Laureate Illya Prigogine once said, "When a system is far from equilibrium, small islands of coherence in a sea of chaos have the capacity to lift the entire system to a higher order."[1] And so it is in our time.

The society we wish for is being built in miniature every day. Countless thousands of people and their communities are finding the means to make a more humane vision of life and society flourish here and now. In a time of crisis, every co-operative or commons that is created is both lifeboat and beacon. Even in the most extreme circumstances and the darkest of times, as in the Syrian inferno, there is light and hope.

Notes

Introduction

1. "Marine Le Pen's Rise in 'Forgotten France,'" April 20, 2017, video, youtube.com/watch?v=N-ooZ96nA8g.
2. Jim Tankersley, Ben Casselman, and Emily Cochrane, "Voters Like Biden Infrastructure Plan: G.O.P. Still Sees an Opening on Taxes," *New York Times*, April 15, 2021.
3. Terrence Des Pres, *The Survivor: An Anatomy of Life in the Death Camps*, Oxford University Press, 1976.

Chapter 1: Treason of the State

1. I owe this term to Andrew Nikiforuk's use of it in his book, *The Energy of Slaves: Oil and the New Servitude*, Greystone Books, 2012.
2. Jason DeParle, *American Dream: Three Women, Ten Kids and a Nation's Drive to End Welfare*, Penguin, 2005.
3. Lucas Pleva, "Texas Congresswoman Eddie Bernice Johnson Says Social Security Slashed Poverty Among the Elderly," Poynter Institute, politifact.com, August 17, 2010.
4. Constitutional Rights Foundation, "BRIA 14 3 a: How Welfare Began in the United States," crf-usa.org.
5. "Bismarck Tried to End Socialism's Grip—By Offering Government Healthcare," Lorraine Boissoneault, Smithsonian.com, July 14, 2017.
6. J. Steinberg, *Bismarck: A Life*, Oxford University Press, 2013.
7. Social Security Administration, "Otto von Bismarck," ssa.gov/history/ottob.html.
8. In Lenin's vision, "*all* citizens" are converted into "workers and employees of a *single* huge syndicate—the entire state—and the complete subordination of the entire work of this syndicate to a genuinely democratic state, to a state of the Soviets of Workers' and Soldiers' Deputies." "There will be "no getting away from it, nowhere to hide." Hence, an exact blueprint for a totalitarian dictatorship. V. Lenin, *The State and Revolution*, 1917.
9. In late November 1859, Engels acquired one of the first 1,250 copies of Charles Darwin's *The Origin of Species* and then sent a letter to Marx

saying: "Darwin, by the way, whom I'm just reading now, is absolutely splendid." The following year, Marx wrote back and confirmed that Darwin's work established the natural-history foundation of his historical materialism: "These last four weeks, I have read all sorts of things. Among others, Darwin's book on natural selection. Although it is developed in the crude English style, this is the book, which contains the basis on natural history for our view." "*Karl Marx, December 19, 1860,*" *The Essential Marx: The Non-economic Writings, A Selection*, New American Library, 1979, 359.

10. It is amusing to note here, in passing, the similarity between this Marxist view of history and Francis Fukuyama's famous claim that the globalization of capitalism is itself the end of history, with capitalism marking the apex and end point of human achievement.

11. James C. Scott, *Against the Grain: A Deep History of the Earliest States*, Yale University Press, 2017.

12. In fifth-century Athens, out of a population of perhaps 400,000, a mere 40,000 males held citizenship. In any discussion of Greek democracy, this should not be forgotten. See Robert Flacelière, *Daily Life in Greece at the Time of Pericles*, Hachette, 1959.

13. Scott, *Against the Grain*.

14. According to Freedom House, in 2018 global freedom was in decline for the thirteenth consecutive year spanning countries in every region. *Freedom in the World 2019: Freedom in Retreat*, freedomhouse.org.

15. "Constitutions which aim at the common advantage are correct and just without qualification, whereas those which aim only at the advantage of the rulers are deviant and unjust, because they involve despotic rule which is inappropriate for a community of free persons," "Aristotle's Political Theory," *Stanford Encyclopedia of Philosophy*, Stanford University, revised November 7, 2017.

16. *World Inequality Report*, World Inequality Lab, 2018.

17. F. Engels, *The Condition of the Working Class in England*, 1845.

18. Ibid.

19. Nancy MacLean, *Democracy in Chains: The Deep History of the Radical Right's Stealth Plan for America*, Penguin Random House, 2017.

Chapter 2: Civil Power and the New Legitimacy

1. The use of the term "male" here is not merely conventional shorthand for "people." Aristotle, like all the early Greek philosophers, treated the male as the true subject of philosophical and political enquiry. Only males were granted rights of citizenship—women and slaves were not formally citizens with inherent political rights.

2. *Aristotle: The Nicomachean Ethics*, David Ross, trans., Oxford University Press, 1980, 208.

3. John Locke, *Second Treatise on Government*, 1689.

4. Adam Ferguson, *An Essay on the History of Civil Society*, 1767; reprint by Garland, 1971.

5. Boris DeWiel, "A Conceptual History of Civil Society: From Greek Beginnings to the End of Marx," *Past Imperfect*, 6, 1997, 3–42.

6. Ibid.

7. Stefano Zamagni, *An Axiological Reorientation of Economic Science*, 2019.

8. Ibid.

9. Dylan Riley, *The Civic Foundations of Fascism in Europe*, Johns Hopkins University Press, 2010.

10. Bauman, Z. (2013), "Europe is trapped between power and politics," *Social Europe Journal*, May 14.

11. Jurgen Habermas, "New Social Movements," *Telos*, 49, 1981, 33.

Chapter 3: The Commons: Dispossession and Reclamation

1. Gauri Noolkar-Oak and Vaibhavi Pingale, "India's Local Water Conflicts Are a Looming Threat," *The Diplomat*, May 16, 2019.

2. T.M. Mukundam, "The Ery Systems of South India," *PPST Bulletin*, Madras, 1980.

3. David Bollier, *Think Like a Commoner*, New Society Publishers, 2014, 34.

4. Guy Shrubsole, *Who Owns England?: How We Lost Our Land and How to Take It Back*, William Collins, 2019.

5. Paul Piff, "Does Money Make You Mean?" TEDTalks, December 20, 2013, video, youtube.com/watch?v=bJ8Kq1wucsk.

6. Simon Fairlie, "A Short History of Enclosure in Britain," *The Land*, No. 7, Summer 2009.

7. Francis Hutcheson, *A Short Introduction to Moral Philosophy*, 1749.

8. Bernard Mandeville, *The Fable of the Bees*, Harmondsworth, 1970, 191, 334.

9. Mandeville, two centuries before Thatcher, was one the originators of the view that there is no such thing as society—only an aggregation of self-serving individuals and families in perpetual competition.

10. International Cooperative Alliance, ica.coop/en/cooperatives/facts-and-figures.

11. John B. Goodman and Gary W. Loveman, "Does Privatization Serve the Public Interest?" *Harvard Business Review*, 69(6), 1991, 26–38.

12. Nicholas Shaxson, "Tackling Tax Havens," *Finance and Development*, 56(3), September 2019.

13. Karol Yearwood, *The Privatised Water Industry in the UK. An ATM for investors*, 2018, Public Services International Research Unit, gre.ac.uk/business/research/centres/public-services/home.

14. E. Chong, F. Huet, and S. Saussier, "Public-Private Partnerships and Prices: Evidence from Water Distribution in France," *Review of Industrial Organization*, 29, 2006, 149–69.

15. "Lack of Water Drives Residents of India's Chennai City to Desperation," Agence France-Press, June 22, 2019, thenationalnews.com.

16. Vandana Shiva, *Water Wars; Privatization, Pollution, and Profit*, South End Press, 2002.

Chapter 4: The Co-operative City

1. Soft Construction with Cooked Beans, 1936.

2. Manuel Castells, *Rupture: The Crisis of Liberal Democracy*, Polity, 2018, 89.

3. Melissa Garcia Lamarca, "Resisting Evictions Spanish Style," *New Internationalist*, April 2013.

4. See in particular, Saul Alinsky, *Rules for Radicals*, 1971.

5. The term "social economy" has undergone a number of transformations, including its most recent formulation as social/solidarity economy (SSE). Here, I am using the terms interchangeably as they are used in both forms by the organizations and case examples I describe.

6. *The Impetus Plan for the Social and Solidarity Economy, 2016–2019*, impetusplan-sse-eng_web.pdf.

7. Public Policies Fostering the Social and Solidarity Economy in Barcelona (2016–2019), UNRISD Working Paper 2020–5, 2020,

8. Amartya Sen, *Development as Freedom*, 1999.

9. Annette Strauss Institute, *What We Do Together, Social Capital Project*, SCP Report No. 1-17, 2017.

10. Ibid.

Chapter 5: The Way of the Peasant

1. John Vidal, "The Seeds of Wrath," *The Guardian*, June 19, 1999.

2. Rahul Tripathi, "NCRB Data Shows 42,480 Farmers and Daily Wagers Committed Suicide in 2019," *Economic Times*, updated September 01, 2020.

3. Maria Elena Martinez-Torres and Peter M. Rosset, "La Via Campesina: The Evolution of a Trans National Movement," *Global Policy Forum*, February 8, 2010.

4. Martinez-Torres and Rosset, Declaration of Quito.

5. Stefano Varese (1996, 62), quoted in Martinez-Torres and Rosset, "La Via Campesina."

6. See Anette Aurelie Desmarais, *La Via Campesina: Globalization and the Power of Peasants*, Pluto Press, 2007, 19.

7. La Via Campesina, "La Via Campesina Relaunches 'Global Campaign for Seeds, a Heritage of Peoples in the Service of Humanity,'" press release, October 16, 2018.

8. Reset, "The Privatisation of Seeds," en.reset.org.

9. Vanadana Shiva, "Seeds of Suicide and Slavery Versus Seeds of Life and Freedom," *Al Jazeera*, March 30, 2013.

10. John Vidal, "The Seeds of Wrath," *The Guardian*, June 19, 1999.

11. P. Sainath, *The Neoliberal Attack on Rural India*, Dossier no. 21, Tricontinental: Institute for Social Research, October 2019.

12. "ETC Group Responds to Purdue U. Promotion of Terminator as Environmental Protector," *Cropchoice*, May 2, 2002.

13. Ann Cooper, with Lisa M. Holmes, *Bitter Harvest: A Chef's Perspective on the Hidden Dangers in the Food We Eat*, Routledge, 2000, 96.

14. Desmarais, *La Via Campesina*.

15. Ibid.

Chapter 6: Deep Democracy in Kerala

1. The name "Syrian Christian" derives from the historical and liturgical connection of the Christian community in Kerala to the rites of the Eastern Orthodox Church in Syria.

2. Described in Samuel Mateer's book, *The Land of Charity: A Descriptive Account of Travancore and Its People, with Especial Reference to Missionary Labour*, Laurier Books, 1991.

3. K. Rajesh, *Participatory Institutions and People's Practices in India: An Analysis of Decentralisation Experiences in Kerala State*, Institute for Social and Economic Change, Bangalore, 2009.

4. Rashmi Sharma, "Kerala's Decentralisation: Idea in Practice," *Economic and Political Weekly*, 38(36), 2003, 3832–50.

5. J. Elamon, R. W. Franke, and B. Ekbal, "Decentralization of Health Services: The Kerala People's Campaign," *Int J Health Serv*, 34(4), 2004, 681–708.

6. M. A. Oommen, "Reform and Economic Change: Experiences and Lessons from Kerala," in B. A. Prakash, *Kerala's Economy: Performance, Problems, Prospects*, Sage, 1994, 117–40.

7. Ibid.

8. A. Mukherjee, "A Quarter of a Million Women in Kerala Earn a Living with Dignity," *Universitas Forum*, 3(1), February 2012.

9. P. Sainath, "Kerala's Women Farmers Rise Above the Flood," *Counterpunch*, September 28, 2018.

10. Ibid.

11. Suneetha Kadiyala, *Scaling Up Kudumbashree: Collective Action for Poverty Alleviation and Women's Empowerment*, International Food Policy Research Institute, Washington, D.C., 2004.

Chapter 7: Living Without Approval: Stateless Democracy in Rojava

1. "Living without approval" is the apt term used by Dilar Dirk in her interview of the same name for the publication *Stateless Democracy*, New World Academy, Reader #5, 2015.

2. The name of ISIS (Islamic State of Iraq and Syria) has changed over the years, from ISIL (Islamic State of Iraq and Lebanon) to IS (Islamic State), to *Daesh*, as it is called by the Kurds in Syria. I am using the term ISIS, which is the one most familiar to readers.

3. In Raqqa, following the expulsion of ISIS, coalition forces were confronted with the ghastly sight of decapitated bodies that had been fitted with the severed heads of other victims.

4. M. Knapp, A. Flach, and E. Ayboga, *Revolution in Rojava: Democratic Autonomy and Women's Liberation in Syrian Kurdistan*, Pluto Press, 2016, 143.

5. *Democratic Confederalism* is often used interchangeably with the term *Democratic Autonomy*, which is also used to describe the philosophy of this system. To avoid confusion, I am using Democratic Confederalism throughout as the application of Democratic Autonomy in the actual governance structures of the region.

6. Abdullah Öcalan, *Democratic Confederalism*, International Initiative, Brochure #2, 2011.

7. *Beyond the Frontline: The Building of the Democratic System in North and East Syria*, Rojava Information Centre, December 2019.

8. Cinar Sali of TEVDEM, M. Knapp, A. Flach, and E. Ayboga, *Revolution in Rojava: Democratic Autonomy and Women's Liberation in Syrian Kurdistan*, Pluto Press, 2016, 87.

9. The seven autonomous administrations are: Democratic Civil Administration of Deir Ezzor, Democratic Civil Administration of Raqqa, Democratic Civil Administration of Tabqa, Democratic Civil Administration of Manbij and its countryside, Democratic Autonomous Ad-

ministration for the Euphrates region, Democratic Civil Administration in the Jazira, and Democratic Civil Administration of Afrin.

10. Rojava Information Center, *Beyond the Frontlines: The building of the Democratic System in North and East Syria*, December, 2019.

11. H. Allsopp and W. van Wilgenberg, *The Kurds of Northern Syria: Governance Diversity and Conflicts*, Bloomsbury, 2019.

12. Enab Baladi, "Kurdish-led SDF Dominates Political Life in Eastern Euphrates," April 23, 2021, english.enabbaladi.net.

Chapter 8: The World Unmasked

1. Umair Haque, "The West's Failure on Covid is Even More Staggering Than You Think," *Eudaimonia*, November 13, 2020.

2. Ibid.

3. *ILO Monitor: COVID-19 and the World of Work, Third Edition, Updated Estimates and Analysis*, International Labour Organization, April 29, 2020.

4. Esmé Berkhout, et al., *The Inequality Virus: Bringing Together a World Torn Apart by Coronavirus Through a Fair, Just and Sustainable Economy*, Oxfam International, January 25, 2021.

5. Carlos Irwin Oronce, et al., "Association Between State-Level Income Inequality and COVID-19 Cases and Mortality in the USA," *Journal of General Internal Medicine*, 35(9), 2020, 2791–3.

6. Chuck Collins, Omar Ocampo, and Sophia Paslaski, *Billionaire Bonanza 2020: Wealth Windfalls, Tumbling Taxes, and Pandemic Profiteers*, Institute for Policy Studies, April 23, 2020.

7. Matt Egan, "America's Billionaires Have Grown $1.1 Trillion Richer During the Pandemic," *CNN Business*, updated January 26, 2021.

8. T. J. Bollyky, et al., "The Relationship Between Democratic Experience, Adult Health, and Cause-Specific Mortality in 170 Countries Between 1980 and 2016: An Observational Analysis," *The Lancet*, April 20, 2019.

9. Geoffrey York, Mark Mackinnon, Nathan Vanderklippe, and Adrian Morrow, "The Notorious Nine: These World Leaders Responded to the Coronavirus with Denial, Duplicity and Ineptitude," *Globe and Mail*, April 21, 2020.

10. Rachel Shabi, "The Pro-Privatization Shock Therapy of the UK's Covid Response," *New York Review of Books*, July 8, 2020.

11. David Hall, et al., *Privatized and Unprepared: The NHS Supply Chain*, University of Greenwich and We Own It, 2020.

12. Sarah Neville, "Pathologists Warn UK Coronavirus Testing Needs 'Urgent' Improvement," *Financial Times*, London, June 10, 2020.

13. Rachel Shabi, "The Pro-privatization Shock Therapy of the UK's COVID Response," *New Cold War*, July 11, 2020.

14. Katherine Eban, "'That's Their Problem': How Jared Kushner Let the Markets Decide America's COVID-19 Fate," *Vanity Fair*, September 17, 2020.

15. Ibid.

16. Ibid.

17. Vaccination rates tell a similar story. Republican states are also ones where the vaccination rates are lowest in the country. According to a poll held in March 2021, Democrats were far more likely to take the vaccine than Republicans were. Among Democrats, 47% said they had already received one dose of the vaccine, whereas just 33% of Republicans said they had. When asked whether they would eventually get the vaccine, 42% of Democrats said yes, compared with 23% of Republicans. See Harry Enten, "Red States Are Vaccinating at a Lower Rate Than Blue States," *CNN Politics*, April 10, 2021.

18. Megan Leonhardt, "Uninsured Americans Could Be Facing Nearly $75,000 in Medical Bills If Hospitalized for Coronavirus," *Make It*, CNBC, updated January 12, 2021.

19. Felicity Lawrence, "UK Hunger Crisis: 1.5m People Go Whole Day without Food," *The Guardian*, April 11, 2020.

20. Nidhi Sharma, "Coronavirus Has a Free Run in Poll States: West Bengal's Only Half Done," *Economic Times*, updated April 15, 2021.

21. "India Covid: Delhi Builds Makeshift Funeral Pyres as Deaths Climb," *BBC News India*, April 27, 2021.

22. Vijay Prashad and Subin Dennis, "An Often Overlooked Region of India Is a Beacon to the World for Taking on the Coronavirus," *MROnline*, March 24, 2020.

23. Yakul Krishna, "A Left Ruled State in India is Leading the Battle Against Coronavirus," *Current Affairs*, April 5, 2020.

24. Rukmini S, "Can New Mortality Data Explain India's Low COVID Death Numbers?" IndiaSpend, March 23, 2021.

25. Peter Kropotkin, *Mutual Aid: A Factor of Evolution*, 1902.

26. crowdfightcovid19.org.

27. gavi.org/covax-facility

28. Stephanie Nebehay, "COVAX Vaccines Reach More Than 100 Countries, Despite Supply Snags," *National Post*, April 8, 2021.

29. George Monbiot, "The Horror Films Got It Wrong: This Virus Has Turned Us into Caring Neighbours," *The Guardian*, March 31, 2020.

Chapter 9: Transformation and Integration

1. Robert Axelrod, *The Evolution of Co-operation*, Basic Books, 1984.
2. Jay Walljasper, *On the Commons*, October 2, 2011.
3. Ibid.
4. James Manyika and Kevin Sneader, "AI, Automation, and the Future of Work: Ten Things to Solve For," McKinsey Global Institute, June 1, 2018.
5. Y.N. Harari, *Sapiens: A Brief History of Humankind*, Harvil Secker, 2016.
6. Shannon Hall, "Exxon Knew About Climate Change Nearly Forty Years Ago," *Scientific American*, October 26, 2015.

Chapter 10: From Welfare State to Partner State

1. Cosma Orsi, *The Value of Reciprocity. Arguing for a Plural Political Economy*, Federico Caffè Centre Publisher and University of Roskilde (DK), 2006.
2. Vasilis Kostakis, *The Political Economy of Information Production in the Social Web: Towards a "Partner State Approach,"* TUT Press, 2011.
3. FLOK Society Project (Free, Libre, Open, Knowledge), Ecuador, 2013.
4. As a member of the FLOK research team, my own work focused on the social economy, state institutions, and the Partner State. See: J. Restakis, "Social Knowledge, the Social Economy, and the ICT Revolution: A Public Policy Quartet," FLOK Society Project, 2014.
5. Michel Bauwens, "Class and Capital in Peer Production," *Capital & Class*, 33(1), January 1, 2009, 121–42.
6. Michel Bauwens and Vasilis Kostakis, "Towards a New Reconfiguration Among the State, Civil Society and the Market," *Journal of Peer Production*, 7, 2015. Accessed January 10, 2020.
7. Stefano Zamagni, *An Axiological Reorientation of Economic Science*, 2019.
8. Ibid.
9. Pat Conaty, Alex Bird, and Phillip Ross, *Not Alone: Trade Union and Co-Operative Solutions for Self-employed Workers*, Co-operatives UK, 2017.
10. C. Borzaga, M. Calzaroni, C. Carini, and M. Lori, "Structure and Performance of Italian Cooperatives," EURICSE and the National Institute of Statistics, 2019, www.euricse.eu.
11. "Fureai Kippu, Barter Based Health Care for Senior Citizens," video, September 4, 2014, youtube.com/watch?v=x7bzk3DmoGk.
12. Michel Bauwens and Vasilis Kostakis, "Towards a New Reconfiguration Among the State, Civil Society and the Market," *Journal of Peer Production*, 7, 2015.

Chapter 11: Civilizing the State: Principles and Policies

1. Bills and Debates in Congress Relating to Trusts, Fiftieth Congress to Fifty Eighth Congress.
2. Michael McLeay, Amar Radia, and Ryland Thomas, "Money Creation in the Modern Economy," Bank of England, *Quarterly Bulletin*, 2014.
3. Thomas Picketty, *Capital in the 21st Century*, Harvard University Press, 2014.

Epilogue

1. Illya Prigogine, "Biographical," *The Nobel Prize*, nobelprize.org.

Index

About the Author

JOHN RESTAKIS has been active in the co-op movement for 25 years. He is the former executive director of Community Evolution Foundation and the BC Co-operative Association. John is co-founder of Synergia Co-operative Institute. A practitioner and pioneering researcher into international co-operative economies, he writes and lectures on economic democracy and the role of co-operatives in humanizing economies. He is the author of *Humanizing the Economy: Co-operatives in the Age of Capital* and lives in Vancouver, B.C.

ABOUT NEW SOCIETY PUBLISHERS

New Society Publishers is an activist, solutions-oriented publisher focused on publishing books to build a more just and sustainable future. Our books offer tips, tools, and insights from leading experts in a wide range of areas.

We're proud to hold to the highest environmental and social standards of any publisher in North America. When you buy New Society books, you are part of the solution!

At New Society Publishers, we care deeply about *what* we publish—but also about *how* we do business.

- All our books are printed on 100% **post-consumer recycled paper**, processed chlorine-free, with low-VOC vegetable-based inks (since 2002). We print all our books in North America (never overseas)

- Our corporate structure is an innovative employee shareholder agreement, so we're one-third employee-owned (since 2015)

- We've created a Statement of Ethics (2021). The intent of this Statement is to act as a framework to guide our actions and facilitate feedback for continuous improvement of our work

- We're carbon-neutral (since 2006)

- We're certified as a B Corporation (since 2016)

- We're Signatories to the UN's Sustainable Development Goals (SDG) Publishers Compact (2020–2030, the Decade of Action)

To download our full catalog, sign up for our quarterly newsletter, and to learn more about New Society Publishers, please visit newsociety.com

ENVIRONMENTAL BENEFITS STATEMENT

New Society Publishers saved the following resources by printing the pages of this book on chlorine free paper made with 100% post-consumer waste.

TREES	WATER	ENERGY	SOLID WASTE	GREENHOUSE GASES
29	2,300	12	100	12,670
FULLY GROWN	GALLONS	MILLION BTUs	POUNDS	POUNDS

Environmental impact estimates were made using the Environmental Paper Network Paper Calculator 4.0. For more information visit www.papercalculator.org

Certified

Ⓑ

Corporation

new society
PUBLISHERS
www.newsociety.com

FSC
www.fsc.org

MIX
Paper from responsible sources
FSC® C016245

SDG PUBLISHERS COMPACT